HEBREW MAN

HEBREW MAN

LECTURES
DELIVERED AT THE INVITATION OF
THE UNIVERSITY OF TÜBINGEN
DECEMBER 1-16, 1952

with an appendix on
JUSTICE IN THE GATE

by

LUDWIG KÖHLER

Translated by PETER R. ACKROYD

SCM PRESS LTD
56 BLOOMSBURY STREET
LONDON

Translated from the German
DER HEBRÄISCHE MENSCH
J. C. B. Mohr (Paul Siebeck), Tübingen, *1953*

334 00608 2
*First published in English 1956
by SCM Press Ltd
56 Bloomsbury Street, London
© SCM Press Ltd 1956
Printed in Great Britain by
Fletcher & Son Limited, Norwich*

To

**ALBRECHT ALT
WALTER BAUMGARTNER**

Two Friends

CONTENTS

	Translator's note	viii
	Preface to the reissue	ix
1	THE PURPOSE OF THE BOOK	11
2	PHYSICAL CHARACTERISTICS	15
3	HEALTH AND SICKNESS	37
4	HOW THE HEBREW LIVED I	61
5	HOW THE HEBREW LIVED II	87
6	HOW THE HEBREW THOUGHT I	115
7	HOW THE HEBREW THOUGHT II	125
8	*Appendix:* JUSTICE IN THE GATE	149
	Index of Authors	177
	Subject Index	179
	Index of Biblical References	183

TRANSLATOR'S NOTE

Biblical quotations follow the text of the Revised Version as far as is practicable, that is, except where the Hebrew text is emended, or where a more exact rendering of the Hebrew is necessary to bring out the point in discussion. Hebrew words are transliterated only approximately, and for these and the above points reference should be made to the Hebrew text and a Hebrew Lexicon for more exact information.

PREFACE TO THE REISSUE

THE enthusiasm with which Professor (now Sir) Godfrey Driver welcomed the original German of this book when it was published in 1953 is worth quoting: 'The interest of this little book is out of all proportion to its size; for Dr Köhler has compressed an immense amount of information into a small space. He describes the life of an ordinary Hebrew man from the physical, psychological, and intellectual points of view : his body in health and ill-health, expectation of life, upbringing, manhood, and death, his attitude to the vicissitudes of life and the spiritual influences forming its background and working on him.'

The English translation of 1956 has been for some time out of print, and its reissue is undertaken in the belief that this introduction to the way of life of the ancient Hebrew still provides an excellent entry into a world so familiar from the long tradition of reading the Old Testament in synagogue and church, but in reality strange and in so many ways different from contemporary life. This is a book to give the reader an insight into what that ancient world felt like to those who lived in it. It is, as any such introductory presentation should be, wisely imaginative, since there are so many points at which our information is deficient. A coherent picture demands the filling of the gaps on the basis of reasonable inference from what we do know.

In the twenty years which have passed since Dr Köhler originally published this book, much has been written which helps to illuminate the subject further. There are points at which his presentation needs modification, particularly on matters of detail. But the main emphasis of the presentation remains valid. It may usefully be supplemented by the wealth of information in R. de Vaux, *Ancient Israel: Its Life and Institutions* (Engl. transl. by J. McHugh, 1961), which includes a considerable bibliography. The wider religious background, providing the context for much that is said about the thinking of the Hebrew, is now conveniently available in H. Ringgren, *Religions of the Ancient Near East* (Engl. transl. by J. Sturdy, 1973), which provides supplementation in particular to the indications of Ugaritic thought in this book. The discussion of the wisdom writings, in particular of Proverbs in Chapter 5 and of Job in the Appendix, may be amplified and modified from R. B. Y. Scott, *The Way of Wisdom in the Old Testament* (1971) and G. von Rad, *Wisdom in Israel* (Engl. transl. by J. D. Martin, 1972). The nature of the Deuteronomic preaching style and its relationship to prophecy may be traced in E. W. Nicholson, *Preaching to the Exiles* (1970). For many of the topics touched on, reference should be made to the *Interpreter's Dictionary of the Bible* (4 vols., 1962) and to recent commentaries (for details, consult an introductory work such as O. Eissfeldt, *The Old Testament: An Introduction* [Engl. transl. by P. R. Ackroyd, 1965], or G. Fohrer, *Introduction to the Old Testament* [Engl. transl. by D. Green, 1968, 1970]).

PREFACE TO THE REISSUE

The text in this reissue is virtually unchanged, though the translator is conscious that it is not always as felicitous as he would like. The one correction of error which Dr Köhler kindly sent before his death in 1956 has been included; the translator (and indeed all those whom he consulted) was so ignorant as to suppose that 'Romansh' was the same as 'gypsy' (p. 67), and did not know that it refers to a particular part of Switzerland. Dr Köhler very properly suggested that it would be as well, if a visit were to be paid to that area, for this piece of misunderstanding to be carefully concealed.

Peter R. Ackroyd

1

THE PURPOSE OF THE BOOK

THE Bible contains a number of notes which were added to make the context intelligible to the reader. We find a geographical note, for example, obviously intended for readers outside Palestine: '. . . the mount of Olives, which is before Jerusalem on the east' (Zech. 14.4). Elsewhere a point of linguistic and cultural interest is noted: 'Beforetime in Israel, when a man went to inquire of God, thus he said, Come and let us go to the Seer: for he that is now called a Prophet was beforetime called a Seer' (I Sam. 9.9). A further linguistic note occurs in Jer. 35.5. Here, in the phrase '. . . bowls full of wine', the word used for 'bowls' (*gābīa‘*) is an Egyptian loan-word, and so the words 'and cups' have been added. The word in the addition (*kōs*) is the normal Hebrew word. Similarly in Isa. 51.17, 22, the rare word *qubba‘at* for cup has been explained by the addition of *kōs*.

As time went on, it became more and more necessary to add such explanations of language and content. They were no longer written in the text itself, but collected together in separate works. Thus there came into existence a special branch of Bible study, Biblical or Hebrew archaeology, which has produced a whole range of writings of different kinds.[1] The nature and variety of this literature, often quite astonishing in its learning, are not here discussed. It is enough to mention the two German works which show both what it can accomplish, and perhaps also its ultimate limitations: Wilhelm Nowack, *Lehrbuch der hebräischen Archäologie* (1894), and Immanuel Benzinger, *Hebräische Archäologie* (third edition 1927).

To us, a later generation (I cannot, at my age, say 'younger' generation), it has become increasingly obvious, when we study these books and others like them, that they suffer from a certain one-sidedness. An

[1] A small random selection may be given here. A beginning was made by the Spanish monk Benito Arias Montano, the librarian of Philip II of Spain, who, together with others, published in Antwerp in 1569-1572 the Antwerp Polyglot, the *Biblia Regia*. On March 3, 1571, he wrote for its eighth volume the introduction to the tractate *Jeremias sive de actione*, on which there followed eight other tractates, and he mentioned John 12.32 f. and 21.18 f. as examples of expressions which need an explanation if they are not to be misunderstood. Theodore of Beza has the merit of having inspired Bonaventure Cornelius Bertramus, Professor of Hebrew in Geneva from 1566 to 1584, to write his little booklet in Ciceronian Calvinistic Latin: *De politica Judaica tam civili quam ecclesiastica, jam inde a suis primordis hoc est ab orbe condito repetita* (1574). Montanus and those who followed him were anxious to understand the Bible. Bertramus and those who followed up the questions he raised, were anxious to depict from the biblical record the secular and spiritual aspects of the community. This second task was long driven into the background by the first. Bertramus's book was itself soon displaced by one by the Bolognese Cavolus Sigonius, the famous teacher of law, whose grave is still shown in Modena: *De re publica Hebraeorum libri septem* (1583), whose rapid reprinting in Frankfurt, Speier, Cologne and elsewhere shows what was in demand. Then follow the treatments of single aspects, of which the following examples may be quoted: Martinus Geier, *De Ebraeorum luctu lugentiumque ritibus* (1656); Johannes Henricus Ursinus, *Arboretum Biblicum* (1663), replaced to-day by a quite differently arranged work by Immanuel Löw, *Die Flora der Juden*, 4 vols. (1928-34), and finally Hadianus Relandus, *Palaestina ex monumentis veteribus illustrata* (1716), out-moded as far as its dates are concerned, but not for its astonishing learning. A broad undertaking, also amazingly rich in material, but unfortunately taking no account of the excavations, is the six (seven) volume work of Gustaf Dalman, *Arbeit und Sitte in Palästina* (1928-39).

THE PURPOSE OF THE BOOK 13

example will show what I mean. Books and articles on the illnesses of the Hebrews certainly provide a comprehensive list of those mentioned in the Old Testament, with conjectures concerning their exact nature. But if we ask what was the general level of health and incidence of disease among the Hebrews, they supply no answer.

We want to picture the Hebrew in all the conditions and experiences of his life. We are not merely concerned with more or less haphazard indications in our texts of what life was like, but, considering all the possibilities, we want to ask: What was it like for the Hebrew in this or that condition? How, for example, does he value life? How does he look upon the experience of death? Does he ever feel depressed? Does physical beauty mean anything to him? How does he feel solitude, or experience fellowship? What does piety mean to him? Johannes Pedersen, in his work *Israel* (Danish edition 1920, English edition 1926 and 1940), has greatly enlarged our insight into a significant part of the Hebrew's psychology and spiritual make-up, and perhaps only the brevity of his *Kulturgeschichte Israels* (1919, E. T. by A. K. Dallas, *History of Hebrew Civilization*, 1926), prevented Alfred Bertholet from following up just these questions, which he was so well equipped to answer.

So the purpose of this book is quite simply to present the Hebrew in all the various aspects of his physical and spiritual life. The great point here is to ask the right questions, to see clearly, and to find the right way of presenting the whole picture. Even a small measure of success in this would clearly be of immediate value. The texts would speak to us more plainly and more fully. We should also be in a better position to make their message plain to others.

The present study is only a preliminary sketch. Others will have to carry the research and the presentation further, and it will not be complete until the Hebrew community, as well as the achievements, economic life, and indeed the whole physical and spiritual experience of the Hebrew, has been fully treated.[1]

[1] L. Köhler, 'Begriff und Gliederung einer Darstellung der Kultur der Hebräer,' *Protestantische Monatshefte* (1917), pp. 135 ff.

2
PHYSICAL CHARACTERISTICS

WHAT did Hebrew men and women look like? How are we to picture them if we want to think about them, or, even more, if we want draw or paint them? An answer frequently given is that the Hebrews belong to the Semitic race. This answer is wrong. In 1781 Schlözer (in Eichhorn's *Repetitorium für biblische und morgenländische Literatur*, Part 8, p. 161) described a number of languages as Semitic, on the basis of Gen. 10, and since then we have been accustomed to speak of Semitic languages. But identity of language and identity of race are not at all the same thing, for while the Negroes of the United States, for example, all speak English, they are not Anglo-Saxon by race. There is in fact no such thing as a Semitic race.

But what of the idea of 'race' itself? It is not a linguistic or psychological concept, but a biological one. A race is a large body of people clearly distinguishable from other such groups by a considerable number of physical and probably also psychological attributes; and it retains all or the majority of these attributes unaltered through many generations. But it must at once be added that, in the historical sphere, races within this clearly defined conception rarely if ever appear. All historical communities are of mixed race.

This is clearly seen, in the case of the Hebrews, in their own tradition. Ephraim and Manasseh both had Joseph as father, but their mother was an Egyptian (Gen. 41.50 ff.). The former tribe was next to Judah in importance—perhaps in reality more important than Judah—and occupied in the historical period almost the whole of central Palestine, while the latter was a small, extraordinarily mobile tribe. Their ancestors were born in Egypt (48.5), but, unlike the younger members of the family to which they belonged, they were attached to Jacob, that is to the Hebrews, 'like Reuben and Simeon' (48.5 f.). Translating this from family history into ethnological terms, it means that these two tribes were by ancestry half Hebrew and half Egyptian, descended from the inhabitants of the eastern delta of the Nile. David and his descendants could trace their ancestry to a Moabitess, as the book of Ruth shows (4.18 ff.). Moses married a Cushite (Num. 12.1), Isaac an Aramaean (Gen. 24), Jacob two Aramaean sisters (Gen. 29.23,28). In the time of Nehemiah, Jews married women from Moab, Ammon and Ashdod (Neh. 13.23 f.). Judah married the 'daughters of a strange god' (Mal. 2.11), and it goes without saying that the invading Hebrews entered into trade and marriage relations with the Canaanites. No further proof is needed. It is not necessary to ask how far the Egyptians of the Delta, the Cushites, Aramaeans, Canaanites, Moabites and others can be differentiated as races, even if we wished to use this term. It is abundantly evident that during the whole of their historical existence (say, from 1200 to 200

B.C.) the Hebrews mingled with other peoples continuously, and almost without compunction.

The same is also true of their descendants. Attempts have been made to draw conclusions concerning the Hebrews from the racial peculiarities of the Jews. But the Jew was never forbidden to marry a woman of another 'race', and Judaism, which is in a most special way both a national and a religious community, has always enjoyed a very considerable mixture of blood.[1] It should not be necessary to say more, but some details show how far from the truth men have sometimes strayed, and what utterly false conclusions have been drawn; so that this may serve as a general warning of the need for caution and restraint.

In statistics the law of large numbers is valid. If you throw a dice marked with one to six points ten, twenty or fifty times, the scores will be a matter of chance. Some sides of the dice will appear often, others rarely or not at all. But if you throw the dice ten thousand times, you will get each side uppermost approximately the same number of times. This is true of the so-called 'Jewish nose', hooked, with a broad point and fleshy nostrils. It is supposed to be typical. Yet in New York three thousand one hundred and ten Jews of both sexes chosen at random were examined. More than half had straight noses, seventeen per cent were pug-nosed, ten per cent flat-nosed, and only thirteen per cent had hooked noses. Moreover, this 'Jewish

---

[1] O. C. Cox, *Caste, Class and Race* (1948); Ruth Benedict, *Race* (revised in 1948); F. Boaz, *Changes in Bodily Form of Descendants of Immigrants* (New York, 1912); M. Fishberg, *Die Rassenmerkmale der Juden* (1913); S. Feist, *Stammeskunde der Juden* (1925).

nose' is also to be found in obviously non-Jewish people.

A comparison has been made of the cephalic index, that is the ratio of the length of the skull to its breadth. Conscription made a division possible between Jews and non-Jews, and the following results were obtained: in Latvia the ratios were 81·05 and 81·88, in Rumania 81·82 and 82·91, in Poland 81·95 and 82·13, in Hungary 82·45 and 81·40, and in Galicia 83·33 and 84·40. These differences are insignificant.

From measurements of height a result was obtained which seemed puzzling at first sight. The Jews in Poland are invariably shorter in stature than those in Rumania. How is this to be explained? The solution is quite simple: the Poles are also just that same amount shorter than the Rumanians. The settlers correspond in stature to the people among whom they live, and it is of course to be noted that height is affected by the standard of living. In Turin the Jews measure on average 5 ft. 4½ in., and Christians 5 ft. 5 in. The average in England is 5 ft. 7½ in., for the standard of living in England is higher than in Turin. Furthermore, in England the average height of Jews and Christians is the same, which means that in England the Jews and non-Jews live in the same social conditions, whereas in Turin they do not. This last factor is, as we shall see, also of importance for the Hebrew.

It has also been claimed that pathological features typical of the Jews have been found. In the Balkans more Christians than Jews are struck by lightning. But the simple explanation is that the Jews there are craftsmen and factory workers, living under the protection of lightning conductors, whereas the Christians are for the most part peasants and foresters away from such protection.

Only one characteristic has been discovered which, after careful examination, has been fully proved to belong to the Jews; they suffer more from psychoses, hysteria and neurasthenia. The reason for this is plain and we shall examine it when we sketch the inner life of the Hebrew. For the present it remains quite clear that we can hardly expect to gain information from the Jews as to the physical appearance of the Hebrews.

There remain three possible sources of information: ancient pictorial representations, excavations, and biblical statements. What can be gathered from these?

As far as pictorial representations are concerned we must make an immediate reservation. We have only a very small number of them,[1] and thus we cannot know whether they really pick out essential features, nor how far the artist was depicting what he actually saw, or was merely reproducing a conventional picture. Furthermore it is the additional features which really determine the impression they make—such things as type of dress, head-coverings, and hair-style. We may have a very clear picture of what a Friesian fisherman looks like, or a man from the Tyrolean alps, or a Spanish bullfighter. But if we imagine pictures of all three, painted naked, who will be able to say for certain which is which?

---

[1] H. Gressmann, 'Die Haartracht der Israeliten', in *Beiträge zur alttestamentlichen Wissenschaft Karl Budde . . . überreicht* (1920), pp. 61 ff. 'There are only three representations of Israelites' (p. 65). A. H. Sayce, *The Races of the Old Testament* (1891) is still worth consulting, but his pictures only show heads, and these are distinguished more by hair-style and head-covering than by anything which can really be called 'characteristics of race'.

Can we then get information from the skeletons discovered in the excavations?

Excavations were carried out at a great many sites in Palestine in the nineteenth century,[1] often at first quite wildly and with eagerness to discover something of real note—and in this proved to be almost without success. Gradually the excavations became more controlled and deliberate, carried through with more awareness of all the possibilities of increasing our knowledge. It is possible that the really important period of excavation still lies in the future. But it is not very likely that this will add to the small amount of significant information which we already possess upon the matter with which we are now concerned. Many graves were unearthed. Various discoveries were made in those which had not already been plundered in earlier times. What information did they give?

On December 8, 1863, de Saulcy found a stone coffin—now in the Louvre[2]—in the Qubur-el-Muluk ('royal graves'), to the north side of Jerusalem. It contained a female skeleton 5 ft. 3 in. long. When the grave was opened, the skeleton fell to pieces, and only the lower jaw, one knee-cap, some finger bones and a shoulder-blade have survived. Fortunately we know the name and date of the dead woman from the inscription on the coffin. Unfortunately, however, this shows that she was Queen Helen of Adiabene, on the border of the Parthian territories, who came over to Judaism in A.D. 48. She was a benefactor to Jerusalem, but she

[1] A brief survey is given by K. Galling, *Biblisches Reallexikon* (1937), pp. 42 ff. The latest information, with valuable criticisms and discussion of the contexts, is to be found in the *Bulletin of the American Schools of Oriental Research*, especially by W. F. Albright.

[2] R. Dussaud, *Les monuments palestiniens et judaïques* (Musée du Louvre, Département des antiquités orientales) (1912), pp. 43 ff.

was not a Hebrew, and does not belong to the Old Testament period.

Since the discovery of this stone coffin, the excavations have brought to light a mass of skeletons and fragments. They belong to almost every century from about 2500 to 100 B.C. and later. They have in the main been described carelessly and without discrimination. For example, in Taanach the list runs: fifteen skeletons, three child skeletons, one complete skeleton of a child of about two years of age, the skull of a child of about ten years, several child-skeletons in jars, sixteen together, none over two years old and the majority new-born; at least eighty items; the skull of a ten-year-old child, the skull of an adult, three male skulls—and so on. It is in this fashion, without careful examination, that the reports of the excavations record the discoveries.

Similarly at Megiddo: six skeletons, two women, three men, one child; the adults estimated to be about 5 ft. 5 in. to 5 ft. 7 in. high; twelve skeletons in a common grave, including two children aged twelve to fifteen; skull bones up to two-fifths of an inch thick, 'but not exceeding the normal in length'. It is obvious how hastily this work has been done. The same style is found all the time: 'remains of two embryo children, a skull-bone with sword wounds, bodies estimated at 5 ft. 7 in. to 5 ft. 11 in. in height'.

One single excavation stands out for its carefulness. This was the one carried out at Gezer by Stewart Macalister, helped by his father, Alexander Macalister, who was an anthropologist.[1] There was a mass grave, with bones which could be seen to belong to various

[1] R. A. S. Macalister, *The Excavation of Gezer*, I-III (1912).

periods, since the burial methods were different. In the lowest stratum the bodies were burnt—a widespread burial custom. The number of individuals cannot now be determined, but there were at least twenty newborn children among them, and at least fifty remains of people over twenty-five years of age, of whom more than half were women. No individual was taller than 5 ft. 7 in., the majority being only about 5 ft. 3¾ in. The skulls were egg-shaped, and thick-boned. The upper stratum contained bodies buried without being burnt. The men averaged 5 ft. 5¾ in. in height, and the women 5 ft. 3 in. In addition there were a few men 5 ft. 11 in. tall. The skull-bones were thin, the face rather long, with the nose projecting sharply; the chins were rounded, and two female skulls had strongly developed lower jaws (prognathism). Have we here the remains of two distinct 'races'? Macalister thinks so, and regards the younger of the two, in the upper stratum, as Amorite. But what is the significance of this suggestion?

On one of the female skeletons, the right arm and shoulder revealed the effects of rheumatism. The weather and general climatic conditions would themselves suggest that many of the inhabitants of Palestine suffered from rheumatic complaints. Here we have the same point indicated by the bones. At the ends of the lower leg-bones is found a thickening like that to be observed in peoples whose normal position for resting is crouching on the heels. The present-day fellahin (peasants) of Palestine reveal, from the observations and measurements which Macalister has made, the same anthropological characteristic which he believed it possible to conclude from the bones he found.

Thus there are a few odd details which attract attention. But what do they really amount to altogether? We are still groping in the dark if we try to draw conclusions from them. Very little, if anything at all, can be concluded from the excavations concerning the physical appearance of the Hebrew.

Let us then endeavour next to discover what can be established or assumed with reasonable probability from general considerations and from the information which the Bible supplies.

1. The Hebrew belongs to a larger group which is to be described as 'Mediterranean man'. As we have already seen, we cannot in this case speak of a 'race' in the strict biological sense. The mixture of blood is much too strong and complex. We are dealing rather with a type of man, known to us from his historical appearance, who is not only to be clearly differentiated from the Negro, the Malay, the Mongol and the Redskin, but also from the European northerner. But this type includes so many different sub-groups—South Italians, Sardinians, Greeks, and also many of the North Africans, Syrians, Arabs, and even some Iranians—that, while it is recognizable, it is also very confused. It is easier to recognize the type from its differences as against other groups, than from its own individual characteristics. The skin is dusky white, that is, browned on a white foundation. The ancient Egyptians were already depicting their men with yellowish colours, but their women white, because the latter lived in the house and so were sheltered from the blaze of the sun.

2. Height is medium; 5 ft. 5 in. to 5 ft. 7 in. may be regarded as the approximate average. This is indi-

cated by the excavated bones, wherever they provide such information; and it can be inferred also from the present-day height of the Mediterranean peoples, and especially of the Palestinians, and further from the quite reliable assumption that food supplies in the ancient world were moderate rather than good.

The Old Testament narratives also point in the same direction. The Hebrews regarded themselves generally as smaller than other peoples. Goliath the Philistine, who was to be defeated by the young David, was six ells (cubits) and a span tall (I Sam. 17.4). This works out to at least eight feet. Saul's height is also recorded as being exceptional. He was, as the English Versions read: '. . . higher than any of the people from his shoulders and upward'. More correctly translated it should read: '. . . as he stood among the people he was a head taller than any of them' (Moffatt, cf. Luther) (I Sam. 10.23). Goliath and Saul were exceptions. General comparisons give a better indication of the position. 'The people is greater and taller than we' was the spies' description of the Canaanites (Deut. 1.28), and this verdict was repeated by others (cf. 9.2, 11.23). 'The Emim . . . a people great, and many, and tall . . .' (2.10); 'and all the people . . . are men of great stature . . . and we were in our own sight as grasshoppers, and so we were in their sight' (Num. 13.32 f.). Isaiah describes the Ethiopians as 'a nation tall and smooth' (18.2, 7), and this is not surprising, for Herodotus also relates that he has heard that they 'are the tallest of all men' (iii.20).

3. Even though the skin colour of the Mediterranean peoples appears dark to us, we must not be led astray by this. For the basic colour is white. It is only pig-

mentation and sun-burn which make it appear dark. In Syria to-day the colour which ranks as best for the human body is 'el-lōn 'el ḥinṭi, the colour of wheat. Wheat in both Hebrew and Arabic gets its name, however, from its colour, which is defined as a mixture of yellow, white, and reddish tints. 'Wheat reddened like the cheeks of a maiden,' says a Palestinian Arab folk-song.[1] 'Reddish' means in the east the colour of the white man in contrast to that of the Negro.

In the story of the birth of the twins Esau and Jacob, Esau is called 'admōni, that is, the reddish brown of the Palestinian lentils, which are called 'ādōm, reddish-brown (Gen. 25.25). The people descended from Esau are thence called 'ĕdōm, the Edomites, or reddish-brown people. The fact that the Hebrews called them this must mean that they thought of themselves as being lighter, more yellowish in colour, or, as we should say, more white. David was 'ruddy, fair-eyed, and good to look upon' (I Sam. 16.12). The story-teller is interested in this, for he repeats it later (17.42). But what does 'ruddy' mean here? It is related that Zwingli was called 'Red Uli' by the rude boys of Zürich; but we no more know of Zwingli than we do of David whether the colour applies to the skin or the hair.

To-day a fair skin ranks as beautiful. In folk-song 'es-sumr, the brown, and 'el-biḍ, the white, are contrasted: 'Go hence, thou brown one, thou pitch of the ships', and 'Go hence, thou white one, soldier's tasty dish' (the longed-for beloved of the soldier). So the shepherd maiden sings in the Song of Songs:

[1] The quotations of songs here and subsequently are from Gustaf H. Dalman, Palästinischer Diwan (1901).

'I am black, but comely, O ye daughters of Jerusalem,
As the tents of Kedar, as the curtains of Solomon.
Look not upon me, because I am swarthy,
Because the sun hath scorched me.
My mother's sons were incensed against me,
They made me keeper of the vineyards;
But mine own vineyard [i.e. her light-coloured skin free from sunburn] have I not kept.' (1.5-6)

The colour of the skin depends upon where the person normally lives. As we have seen, the Egyptians painted the uncovered parts of the body yellow for the men, but whitish for the women, who were always indoors in the shade.

4. The hair is black or dark brown; straight not curly; and long. *'Esh qullak 'alla lēlak* 'what shall I say of thy night' (the array of thy black hair) runs the modern folk-song. The Song of Songs says: 'His locks are bushy, and black as a raven' (5.11); and 'Thy hair (O beloved) is as a flock of (black) goats, that lie along the side of mount Gilead' (4.1, 6.5). Even men wear their hair long. The barber is certainly known, who shaves it right off, as still to-day in Arabia and China and elsewhere, but not the hair-dresser, who trims it stylishly. Samson wears his in seven plaits (not locks, as the biblical translators say), and Delilah weaves his plaits into the web of her flat loom (Judg. 16.13-14). Bedouin still wear such plaits to-day.[1] 'When the hair flowed free in Israel' is the most probable translation of the opening of the ancient Song of Deborah (Judg. 5.2). When one goes into battle, one loosens the plaits and lets the hair hang loose, for knots and binding up

---

[1] J. J. Hess, *Von den Beduinen des Innern Arabiens* (Zürich, 1938), gives as the frontispiece the head of 'Ötebi Muhidz with six plaits on each side of the head.

of the hair might well contain magic and curses. In this we may see the magical significance of the hairstyle. Later, plaits seem to have fallen out of use, or at least we do not hear of them any longer. But Absalom still had his hair cut only once a year, and it then weighed seven pounds (II Sam. 14, 26; only half this weight according to the Greek translation). In Ezekiel (i.e. about 570) we read that the priests must neither have themselves shaved bald nor let their hair grow freely. They are ordered to have a short style (44.20). If any one takes upon himself a special vow, he must avoid the use of the razor, and let the hair of his head grow freely (Num. 6.5). Further, the priests may not wear their hair loose in time of mourning (Lev. 10.6).

5. The beard plays a special rôle. Ancient pictures, as well as present-day conditions, allow us to assume that its growth was sparse. The luxuriant full beard of the Assyrian rulers is due to art, not nature; such a beard was put on, not grown.[1] A beard, more exactly the imperial (chin-tuft) as distinct from the moustache, was called *zāqān* in Hebrew. With this is connected the adjective *zāqēn* which must therefore mean 'bearded'. But the word is also used in a different way. 'From the youth to the bearded man' means the same as 'from the youth to the old man' (Jos. 6.21). 'Job died as a bearded man and full of days' (42.17) obviously means 'as an old man'. 'The bearded men of that city' does not really mean, as is normally said, the eldest men

---

[1] This is true particularly for the Egyptian ornamental beards (Erman, *Ägypten und ägyptisches Leben im Altertum*, revised by H. H. Ranke (1923), p. 252). B. Meissner, *Babylonien und Assyrien* (1920, 1925) does not know of such a custom in that area, but here too the luxuriance and the stylizing of the beards supports this assumption.

of that city, but the citizens who have attained to maturity of life. In short, while it is true that bearded means the same as old, there was probably, as formerly in China, an age limit. Before reaching this age, the chin was shaved; afterwards, the beard was allowed to grow. Every man did the same. This is a matter of hair-style, of the care of the body.

Normally the hair turned grey. The grey-head (Deut. 32.25) means the old man. Egyptians and the inhabitants of Central Arabia dye it early. Hair on the hands was undesirable. Esau was noted for this (Gen. 27.23), whereas Jacob is called a 'smooth man' (27.11).

6. The Hebrew's build is slim, but muscular. This can be inferred from the excavated bones. Manner of life and occupation also suggest the same thing. Our practice of sitting for hours on end on a hard chair, bent over a desk, is unknown. The long garments, worn hung from the shoulders, also encourage an upright position. Even more does the custom of carrying loads on the head. Every day the women and girls walked home from the well with their full water jars on their heads, and they walked proudly and upright. Anyone who travels in Italy notices that even plain Italian women draw attention to themselves by their upright stance, and the Italian man, whether he stands, crouches or lies stretched out, holds himself indolently and yet nobly ('relaxed', as we say). The fact that it was usual to go barefoot may also have contributed to this upright bearing. The Hebrew too was aware of it. 'May thy days be as thy rolling gait' is said of Asher (Deut. 33.25).

Slimness is the result of the moderate, and, more

often, no doubt, rather scanty diet. Muscular development is revealed when Elijah, admittedly in a state of prophetic ecstasy, ran before Ahab's chariot from Carmel to Jezreel, a journey of several hours (I Kings 18.46). Fifty years ago, such a royal runner could still be seen rushing through the main streets of Cairo before the galloping horses of the court carriages. 'The strong has strong legs' (Ps. 147.10). The hero is a runner (Joel 2.7), and Azahel was as swift as a gazelle (II Sam. 2.18). 'They were swifter than eagles, they were stronger than lions, unfailing in strength' (II Sam. 1.23). These are not just empty words of praise which do not correspond to reality. The Hebrew women bear their children so unexpectedly, easily and freely, that the children are already born when the midwife gets to them (Ex. 1.19). King Ahab, mortally wounded in battle, allowed himself to be driven out of the fray, but held himself upright in the chariot until he died in the evening, and lost so much blood that the bottom of the chariot was filled with it (I Kings 22.34 f.). Samson met a young lion on the road—lions were still to be seen in Palestine in 1850, and the Old Testament is full of pictures of lions which derive from actual experience—and he tore the young beast, 'and he had nothing in his hand' (Judg. 14.5 f.). This is not just a mythological feature of the story, for even the youthful David attacked lions and bears and killed them (I Sam. 17.34-36), Benaiah, son of Jehoiada, found a lion which snowfall had driven into a cistern, and climbed down into the cistern and killed it (II Sam. 23.20).

A people would not know of such things if it had not experienced them, and would not relate such details if it did not take pleasure in them. From the time of the Exile onwards (from the middle of the sixth century), the picture changes, at least in part. The town and the workshop, the school and the synagogue do not, it is true, occupy the whole of life. The majority of the Hebrews still live from agriculture, with its strenuous physical work in the open air, but there begins to come to the fore the less strenuous life of handcraft, and more particularly the work of the scribe, which do not exercise the body. This is expressed also in the ideals of the time. Of David, in about 1000 B.C., it is said that he was 'cunning in playing (the harp), a man of substance, accustomed to warfare, prudent in speech, and a comely person, and the LORD is with him' (I Sam. 16.18). That is the Hebrew peasant ideal—six qualities. A man must be musical, for anyone who cannot contribute anything to good company is not of much value. He must have property—this point has been misunderstood by almost all the commentators. Possessions matter to the peasant. A man who has earned nothing and put nothing aside for a time of need (Luke 12.19) has achieved nothing. Whoever has nothing, is nothing, a pauper. A man must be able to fight, to strike down his opponent in battle. Here we sense the utter contempt for everything sickly, weakly and suffering. Jesus was the first to teach a new standard in this. A man must be skilled in speech, for the Hebrew is a member of the Hebrew covenant community and bears responsibility for it. He must be able to present his own case, and plead that of the widow, of the fatherless and of the kinsman under his protection. In all the conversations preserved in the Old Testament, there is never a phrase which is unskilfully expressed, or inapposite, never one which has not its own characteristic nuance. A man should be good-looking, literally, 'a man who looks something'. One might compare the καλὸς κἀγαθός 'presentable and virtuous' of the Greek ideal, which represents basically the same idea, equally pitiless yet not without its value. A man who does not 'look something' is not worth much. Last of the six ideal qualities is the demand that a man should so be, or rather so live, that it will be said of him 'Yahweh is with him'. Every man falls into one of two groups. Either he prospers or he does not. For the one everything succeeds, whether he sows or reaps, hunts or tends his cattle, buys or sells, woos or begets. Such a man has a prosperous touch, good fortune is on his side, he is skilful and resourceful, he has God with him—and the Hebrew says this, and means it quite simply and literally, and by no means in smug piousness. For the other—with him is no Yahweh, or rather Yahweh is not with him, his part is misfortune and mistake, disappointment and failure. What more need be said? It is wiser not even to speak of such men, let alone be in company with them. These six characteristics present us with an ancient peasant ideal, practical, and, as we have seen, hard, lacking in sympathy, but healthy, powerful and vital.

The second picture of an ideal comes to us from about the year 200 B.C. It is likewise an ideal of youth—young men, without blemish, of fine appearance, endowed with all wisdom, of good understanding and quick in the uptake (Dan. 1.4). Attention to good appearance, and freedom from defect have remained, but otherwise everything is directed towards capacity to learn. The book has taken the place of the open field, knowledge has replaced practical ability.

7. Let us return again to the physical appearance of the Hebrew. A list of qualities for the girl or young woman, similar to that which we have seen for the young man, is never gathered together, and what is related, for example, in the Song of Songs, the love song, of physical attractions need not here be set out. Just one question may be raised, and two hints given.

Was the Hebrew thin or fat? We shall see later that the quantity and quality of the food was on the whole rather meagre. This would suggest thinness. It is also possible to start from the ideals described. This is expressed in the choice of names. A favourite name for a girl is Tamar. The bold daughter-in-law of Judah bore this name (Gen. 38.6), so did Absalom's unfortunate sister (II Sam. 13.1), and so also his daughter (II Sam. 14.27). Of both these latter it is said that they were beautiful. The significance of the name Tamar, given to the child to express a wish for her, is seen in the Song of Songs (7.7 f. [Heb. 8 f.]):

> 'O thou beloved, daughter of delights,
> This thy stature is like to a palm tree.'

In the same way Odysseus praises Nausicaa:

> 'Only in Delos have I seen the like, a fresh young palm-tree shooting up by the altar of Apollo . . . for no lovelier sapling ever sprang from the ground. And it is with just the same wonder and veneration that I look at you, my lady.' (6.162-68: E.T. by E. V. Rieu.)

The same comparison is found in Egypt (where the

beautiful woman is called 'a palm of love'), and in the ancient Arab poets. Thus the meaning of the name Tamar—palm—is clear. But what does it actually signify? Contrasted with it is the name Miriam, pronounced Mariam by the Hebrews, from which the Greeks produced the form which we know to-day as Mary. This name has been interpreted as 'child of desire', or, comparing the Egyptian, as 'darling'. But the correct interpretation is probably 'plump', and the name Zobeba (I Chron. 4.8) probably means 'fat'.

The first hint which I wish to mention here indicates a conclusion which may be drawn from what we might call the 'spoken story'. In its opposite, the 'written story', of which there are innumerable examples, all the observations necessary for the understanding of the story are included in the actual text. But there is a series of stories, which unfortunately have never been examined connectedly, in which these observations are missing, particularly at the point where the subject of the verb changes. Gen. 24.30-34 may be mentioned as an example. These passages cannot be understood unless we think of a story-teller. By lively changes of expression, by turning his gaze, by signs with his head, and by movements of his hands to and fro, he makes clear of whom he is speaking, or who is speaking or acting in the story. This liveliness of expression and gesture, which always seems to us as reserved Northerners a characteristic of the Southerner, must be added to what has already been said if we are to have a picture of the physical appearance of the Hebrew. For the impression which a man or group of men gives us depends so much more upon movements, gestures, and the whole of his behaviour than upon his physical appearance alone.

Another hint is necessary to conclude this section, and goes beyond merely physical impressions into the realm of ethics, and even, if you like, of dogmatics. The Old Testament knows and enjoys the concept of beauty, and even of physical beauty. It is not necessary to turn to the Song of Songs in order to appreciate this. Joseph was 'comely and well-favoured' (Gen. 39.6), and so was David (I Sam. 17.42), Sarah (Gen. 12.11), Rachel (Gen. 29.17), Tamar, the daughter of Absalom (II Sam. 14.27), Bathsheba, the wife of Uriah (II Sam. 11.2), Vashti, the Queen of Persia (Esth. 1.11), who refused to disclose her beauty to strange men, and her successor Esther the Jewess (2.7). So also was the king of Ps. 45 (v. 2 [Heb. v. 3]), and Daniel and his companions, although they refused to partake of wine and meat (Dan. 1.8-15). Only the 'servant of the Lord' had 'no form nor comeliness', and therefore 'we esteemed him not' (Isa. 53.2 f.). It was for this reason that the Middle Ages produced the crucifix as a picture of misery. When the first page of the Bible says that man was made in the image of God—the foundation passage for the idea of *imago dei* (Gen. 1.26)—it refers primarily to his upright stature, which distinguishes him from the animals.[1] The starting point is an aesthetic attitude. Man is beautiful, by the will of God. Whoever is beautiful bears in himself the sign of God's good pleasure. We may think of the heavy cloud which thus weighs upon all that is deformed. It was the outlook

---

[1] L. Köhler, 'Die Grundstelle der Imago-Dei-Lehre', *Theologische Zeitschrift*, 4 (1948), pp. 16 ff. The view of Ovid (*Metamorph*, i.85 f.) may be traced back to the Greeks (e.g. Xenophon, *Memor*. 1.4, 11). The matter is worth investigating.

of the Gospel which first lifted that cloud. But it is good to think also of the value which the Old Testament attributes to beauty of appearance, in spite of all the dangers which it brings with it. It is not right to overlook this beauty, or to pay no heed to the obligations it brings.

3

HEALTH AND SICKNESS

(*a*) *Voluntary mutilation of the body.* Whereas illness and death, and the natural duration of life, are almost entirely outside the control of man, there are a number of operations performed on the body which are undertaken completely of his own free will.

The best known and most striking of these among the Hebrews is male circumcision. A similar operation for women is not found among the Hebrews, though it is not unknown among other peoples.[1] Circumcision, which is still practised to-day among the Jews, was very widespread in the ancient world. It is known among the Egyptians and many African peoples, but also in South America, Polynesia and elsewhere. Did the Hebrews adopt this custom from the Egyptians? It is traced back to Abraham, who was explicitly ordered by God to perform it. All the boys in Abraham's household, and among his descendants, and also the slaves, whether born in the household or bought for money, were to be circumcised at the age of eight days (Gen. 17.1-14). This is a late narrative, belonging to the sixth century, and it was in this century, when the Jewish community was in exile among the Babylonians, who did not practise circumcision, that the ancient popular

---

[1] H. H. Ploss, *Das Weib in der Natur- und Völkerkunde* (ninth edition 1908), I, pp. 261 ff. (E. T. *Woman* ... (1935))

custom became a mark of religious distinction. Circumcision, regular times of prayer, the observance of the sabbath, fasts, careful distinction between permitted ('clean') and forbidden ('unclean') foods, and teaching from the scriptures in houses of instruction (synagogues), all became the real signs of membership of the religious community at this time, and remained so thereafter, for Jews who were deprived of the temple and its sacrificial services. No doubt it was at this period that the time appointed for circumcision was moved to the first few days of a boy's life.

Circumcision consists in the removal of a small piece of skin on the male member. It was done with stone (flint) knives (Ex. 4.25, Josh. 5.2), and this too is an indication of its very ancient origin. Its original purpose seems to have been a sexual one,[1] and for this reason it was carried out on adults. It was thus one of the many rites performed on a young man before he entered upon marriage. When the people of Shechem wished to enter into marriage relations with Jacob's people, they had to submit to circumcision. When they, obviously adults, were suffering from fever as a result of the operation, they were hewn down (Gen. 34). Ishmael was thirteen years old when Abraham circumcised him, and Abraham himself was ninety-nine years old when he was circumcised (Gen. 17.24 f.). The people in the time of Joshua were adult (5.2 ff.), and so were those who submitted to circumcision in order to join in the eating of the Passover (Ex. 12.43-49). The newly-married man (whom Ps. 19.5 [Heb. 6] describes as coming happy from the inner room after the wedding-night) is called the ḥāthān. Originally the

[1] *Orientalistische Literaturzeitung*, 31 (1928), Col. 203.

word meant 'one who has been circumcised', as the Arabic form shows. Ḥōthēn now means one who has a son-in-law (a daughter's husband: 'Jethro, who has Moses as his son-in-law', Ex. 18.1). But originally it meant 'one who circumcises'—who performs the operation upon his future son-in-law.

All this was later relegated to the background. The purpose of the custom was forgotten, and magical, religious, or symbolical interpretations replace its original meaning. Thus Jeremiah speaks of a circumcision of the heart (4.4). The time of practising the rite is brought forward, and as a result its connection with marriage is lost. What was once a folk-custom, which enabled the alien people of the Philistines to be branded as the 'uncircumcised' (cf. the complaint of Samson when thirsty, Judg. 15.18), becomes the sign of membership of a confessional unit or religious community. Had it not been for Paul, what might not have happened? For the earliest Christian church seriously thought of making circumcision the absolute condition of entry into the fellowship (Gal. 2).

Castration also occurs in the Old Testament. This practice lasted in court circles into the seventeenth and eighteenth centuries of our era, being performed on singers to prevent their voices breaking, and was normal in the Near East for the guardians of the women's apartments, who played an important rôle and often exercised great influence. In the Old Testament two forms are found (Deut. 23.1 [Heb. 2]). Castrated persons are excluded from the community— which proves that they existed. An earlier error of understanding may here be corrected. It used to be thought necessary to render the Hebrew word *sārīs* as eunuch, because its derivation was wrongly described. It really means simply a court official (Akkadian *sha rēshi*—one who is at the head, the supervisor). Only where his functions demanded it—as for the guardian of the women's apartments (Esth. 2.3, 14 f., 4.4 f.)—is the *sārīs* a eunuch. Moreover, even the latter, in spite of the older statement (Deut. 23.1 [Heb. 2]), is to be a member of the community in the age of salvation (Isa. 56.3 f.). It is not known how ancient castration was among the Hebrews. It came in any case from other cultures and was probably rare.

In time of mourning it was customary to scratch the face, the upper arms and the breast. This was done particularly by the mourning women, if the dead man was a man of note and they were well paid. The law of Solon and the twelve tables of Roman law forbid these self-mutilations.[1] The Hebrew law also forbids such tearings of the skin 'for the sake of the dead', and also the shaving of the forehead for the same purpose (Deut. 14.1).

The priests of Baal on Mount Carmel 'cut themselves after their manner with knives and lances, till the blood gushed out upon them' (I Kings 18.28). This was a Canaanite custom. But the Hebrew ecstatic prophets must have practised the same things. For the time will come when if a prophet is asked 'What are these wounds on thy breast?', he will not wish to admit to ecstatic self-mutilation and will give as his excuse: 'I was wounded in the house of my friends' (Zech. 13.6).

---

[1] A very good survey of mourning customs is provided by Hedwig Jahnow, *Das hebräische Leichenlied im Rahmen der Völkerdichtung* (1923), pp. 2 ff.

(b) *Duration of life among the Hebrews.* Even those who know nothing about the Old Testament know about Jonah in the whale's belly, and about Balaam's ass, and about the impossibly high figures given for the length of life in the earliest times. What are we to make of these figures? Adam lived nine hundred and thirty years, Seth nine hundred and twelve, Enosh nine hundred and five, Kenan nine hundred and ten, Mahalalel eight hundred and ninety-five, Jared nine hundred and sixty-two, Enoch three hundred and sixty-five, Methuselah nine hundred and sixty-nine—hence the saying 'as old as Methuselah' (or Methuselum). (All these figures come from Gen. 5.) Lamech attained seven hundred and seventy-seven years (Gen. 5.31), and Noah nine hundred and fifty (Gen. 9.29). These are the ten patriarchs from the creation to the flood in the six hundredth year of Noah's life (7.6). Since in each case the father's age at the time of the birth of his eldest son is given, and all the above names, after Seth, are those of eldest sons, it is possible to calculate from these figures the number of years from the creation to the flood. Thus this genealogy serves a chronological purpose.[1]

These very large figures have always caused difficulty, but only recently has anyone dared to attempt

[1] This chronology is designed to fit a quite definite eschatological theory. For if these figures are followed, it appears that the Exodus from Egypt took place in the year 2,666 after the creation of the world (Ex. 12.40, together with Gen. 11.10-32, 21.5, 25.26, 47.9, 28). The number 2,666 is not accidental, but is exactly two-thirds of 4,000, as near as may be expressed in whole numbers. Four thousand is four times a thousand (years), and thus equals a complete aeon. (According to another system, an aeon equals six times one thousand years plus one thousand. This other system underlies Gen. 1.1-2.4.) When the end of the 4,000 years comes—in biblical chronology in about the year 200, the time of the Maccabees and of the book of Daniel, the great crisis will occur and the new world will begin.

some kind of interpretation of them. The suggestion is still made by some that these years are not meant to be years of twelve months, but that here one month is called a year. It is then a simple matter of dividing by twelve in order to arrive at our years, and this makes Adam about seventy-seven, Methuselah about eighty, and Noah not quite eighty. These are quite 'reasonable' figures. But this will not work, for since it is also necessary to divide by twelve the numbers indicating the years of birth of the sons, we find that Adam became a father when only just over ten years old, Enosh was only seven and a half, and Mahalalel was not even six. This is clearly unsatisfactory. Nor can the matter be satisfactorily solved if the expedient is tried of saying that the duration of life is expressed in years equal to one month, whereas the age at the birth of the eldest son is expressed in years of twelve months. For then Jared, for example, attained an age of just over eighty years, and had his first son at the age of one hundred and sixty-two, eighty-two years after his death. The figures must therefore stand just as they are, and be regarded as unhistorical and mythological. They are an echo of Babylonian mythological history, in which the primeval kings attained much greater ages.

The excavations, with their large numbers of bodies of children, show a high rate of infant mortality, and this is confirmed by general considerations of public hygiene, and comparative figures from lands in which the conditions are similar to those in which the Hebrews lived. Whereas among us about ten in one thousand children die in the first two years of life, the number amounts to hundreds in the East, in Africa, and so, also, in all probability, in Israel. There is then a special meaning in the words of God found in the prophet: 'I have caused to grow and brought up children' (Isa. 1.2). Even when a man has several wives, the number of children whom he sees grow up and survive him is not large. Marcus Aurelius had thirteen children, but the majority of them died young. Sultan Murad III (1574-95) had one hundred and two children, but at the time of his death there were only twenty sons and twenty-seven daughters still living. The wives and children of these two men lived under favourable conditions.[1] Thus the words 'cause to grow up' have a special significance. In a Hebrew clan or large family someone would be sure to die almost every year, and death wears quite a different appearance—almost an everyday familiarity—from that which it assumes in our small, separate families, where death is rarer and therefore less familiar and perhaps more terrifying.

In addition to those details from the earliest period which we have already noticed, the Old Testament contains a number of others which are within the range of the longevity with which we are familiar. Moses lived to be one hundred and twenty (Deut. 34.7), Joshua one hundred and ten (Josh. 24.29), and Aaron one hundred and twenty-three (Num. 33.39). These may well be figures which have been artificially worked out and graded. But the statement that Eli lived ninety-eight years (I Sam. 4.15) has no such artificiality. Caleb lived at least eighty-five years (Josh.

---

[1] The first of these facts is given in F. Poulsen, *Römische Kulturbilder*, p. 83; the second in Sven Larsen, *Neue Zürcher Zeitung* (1949), No. 1099.

14.10), and Barzillai, who was eighty years of age when he came to the help of the fugitive David, is described as being 'very old' (II Sam. 19.32 [Heb. 33]).

Furthermore, we have statements which do not impress us by their high figures. Rehoboam fifty-eight years of age, Jehoshaphat sixty, Joram, his son, forty (LXX seventy), Ahaziah twenty-three (LXX forty-three), Amaziah fifty-four, his son Azariah sixty-eight, his son Jotham forty-one, his son Ahaz thirty-six, his son Hezekiah fifty-four, his son Manasseh seventy-seven, his son Amon twenty-four, his son Josiah thirty-nine (LXX forty-nine). (These details are found in I Kings 14.21 to II Kings 22.1.) This means that for twelve individuals, who lived one after the other in a period of over five hundred years, the average age was just over forty-seven (LXX just over fifty-two). The eldest lived to be seventy-seven, the youngest twenty-three (or LXX forty-three) or twenty-four. What is even more remarkable is the fact that in a series running through seven generations, father to son, and covering more than three hundred and thirty-nine years (Amaziah to Josiah) the average age is something over forty-eight years, the eldest being seventy-seven and the youngest twenty-four. In I Sam. 2.31 f. a family is mentioned in which no man is to live to old age, for there is a curse upon it. A similar case is found in II Sam. 3.29, for in the family of Joab there is never to be lacking men who have an issue of blood, suffer from skin disease or paralysis, who die a violent death, or have nothing to eat.

We may also attempt to draw conclusions about length of life from general statements, and from statements about age of entry into certain stages of life.

'Yet shall his days be an hundred and twenty years' is what Gen. 6.3 says of man, and this was the traditional age of Moses. 'The number of man's days at the most are a hundred years' says Ben Sira (Ecclus. 18.9). A greater reduction is found in Ps. 90.10: 'The days of our years are threescore years and ten, or even by reason of strength fourscore years'. But in the time of salvation the length of life will increase again. 'The youngest shall die an hundred years old, and he who does not attain an hundred years, shall rank as stricken by a curse' (Isa. 65.20, in amended form, with omission of *ben*). In Num. 4.3, it is laid down that a Levite should begin his service at the age of thirty, and at fifty years of age his period of duty ends. Obviously he is then old, and performs only subsidiary duties (8.26). Elsewhere, the age of beginning is twenty-five years (Num. 8.24), or even twenty (I Chron. 23.24). These are no doubt adjustments made in times when there were insufficient Levites, for here there is also no upper age limit, clearly for the same reason.

According to Num. 14.29 and 32.11, all Israelites who were already twenty years of age and over were to die before the entry into the promised land, for they had murmured against God in their lack of faith. Therefore, since they were to die and not come into Palestine 'your sons shall be herdsmen in the wilderness forty years, and atone for your unfaithfulness, until your carcases be consumed in the wilderness' (14.33). This assumes that they will not pass the age of sixty. It is also to be noted here that it is regarded as a matter of course that men of twenty should already have sons.

Lev. 27.1-8 contains the requirements for vows,

which are to be calculated according to the estimated value of each individual.

From one month to five years, a boy is worth	5	shekels
a girl	3	,,
From five to twenty years, a man is worth	20	,,
a woman	10	,,
From twenty to sixty years, a man is worth	50	,,
a woman	30	,,
Over sixty years, a man is worth	15	,,
a woman	10	,,

Thus human life is divided into five stages; up to one month, from one month to five years, from five to twenty, from twenty to sixty, and then simply over sixty, without any upper limit. Here too it is reasonable to assume that the average expectation of life is fixed at sixty years, and no doubt this corresponds to actual experience. In this, too, the woman is valued throughout at less than the man, but whereas up to five years, and from twenty to sixty, she has two-thirds of his value, she has only half from five to twenty. But after sixty years she loses only twenty shekels in value, while the man loses thirty-five. This proves that we have here not a theoretical valuation, but one which depends upon actual experience. For what value has an old man? And how valuable it is to have in the household an aged mother or aunt!

(c) *Health and Sickness.* We are not here concerned with enumerating the names of diseases which have been preserved in the Bible, and with discussing the derivation and meaning of these names, but rather with a general picture of the place occupied in the life of the Hebrew by health and sickness, and with a few particularly noteworthy details.

It is not easy to answer the question as to whether on the whole man to-day enjoys better health than man in the ancient world. A number of the diseases of antiquity have disappeared, or have largely receded —real leprosy, the plague, and smallpox, for example. In their place other diseases have come to the fore, for diseases, too, have their times and their history, or have more serious consequences as a result of changes in general conditions which do not produce only benefits for man. The number of accidents, for example, is undoubtedly much increased by modern technical advances. Public hygiene has clearly very greatly improved, and the marvellous development of medical science has provided us with ways and means both of guarding against and of curing diseases, so that we are almost tempted to ask how, without them, men of earlier periods did not just die out completely. But in such matters the situation is so enormously complicated that we must reckon with changes of condition which may perhaps never be completely described. A history of the health and sickness of mankind can probably never be written. We cannot get much further than gathering together individual pieces of information and observations. If we add that modern medical knowledge has recognized and adequately described a whole series of diseases about which the ancient world knew nothing, although they were then in existence; and that the judgment as to what is health and what sickness is a subjective one which changes from century to century, that is more than enough of general observation for the present purpose.

We must, however, point out here that the Old Testament contains no expression of opinion at all as to what is healthy and what sick. The individual may indeed ask: Why am I ill? but no one ever asks: What is disease? Why is there such a thing as disease? Furthermore, the language of illness is very little developed. The critical, searching spirit which enabled the Greeks to be the first doctors of mankind, is here lacking. The general word for sickness is ḥŏlī, which means: weakness, looseness. Health is thus strength, or power. This, as we can see, is a concept derived directly from the practical demands of everyday life.

Let us begin with the complaints of old age. Moses, in spite of the great age to which he attained, remained quite free from these. 'His eye was not dim, nor his natural force abated' (Deut. 34.7). Normally it is the eyesight which weakens with age. Isaac had to feel in order to distinguish his sons the one from the other (Gen. 27.21); Jacob, too, no longer saw clearly (48.10); and so also Eli (I Sam. 3.2) and Ahijah, the prophet (I Kings 14.4). The legs lose their strength to carry a man (Zech. 8.4). Old men and women sit in the open places in the sun. David in his old age suffered from persistent coldness. Bedclothes no longer kept him warm through the night. So a young woman was put into his bed, but he did not have intercourse with her (I Kings 1.1-4). This is an expression of a persistent belief that the life-breath of young people is particularly warm and powerful, and can be transferred and so prolong life. In Ecclesiastes we find a melancholy description of old age in the picture of the failing watchman (the arm), the strong men (the legs), the grinding women (the teeth), windows (eyes), mill (voice), and the blossoming of the almond-tree (white hair). It is the time of life when 'evil days come, and the years draw nigh, when thou shalt say, I have no pleasure in them' (12.1-6). The expression 'full of days' can thus be understood.

From the complaints of old age, we may turn to the phenomena connected with birth. Childlessness is the great disaster. Sarah was childless, until God performed a miracle (Gen. 11.30). So too was Rachel in the first years of her marriage, and the distress which she felt is expressed in her cry: 'Give me children, or else I die!' (Gen. 30.1). Even in the New Testament we find the statement: 'But she shall be saved through the childbearing' (I Tim. 2.15). Sarah, Rachel, and also Leah, when unable to bear children, adopted the identical expedient. They gave their husbands their bondmaids, whose children would then be reckoned as their own (Gen. 16.1 f., 30.1-4, 9-13). Samson's mother was barren until God had pity on her (Judg. 13.2), and so also was Hannah, afterwards the mother of Samuel, who, on this account, had to suffer much from her more fortunate co-wife (I Sam. 1.1-7). Michal, Saul's daughter and David's wife, 'had no child unto the day of her death' (II Sam. 6.23), obviously because she expressed herself unfavourably on the subject of David's exposing himself when he danced before the Ark; in other words, as a punishment. For childlessness is not merely a distress for the woman, it is also a punishment, as it was for the women of Gerar (Gen. 20.17 f.). It is the outpouring of the wrath of God. Rebecca too was childless, but when Isaac prayed, she had twins (Gen. 25.21 ff.). Similarly, the Shunamite woman, married to an elderly man, ceased to be barren as a divine reward for her hospitable reception of the prophet and his servant (II Kings 4.8-17). 'Children are a gift of God' (Ps. 127.3).

If we had more information on the point, we should certainly know a good deal concerning all sorts of cultic and other practices by which women who were desirous of children sought to find help in their distress. We only know of prayer, pilgrimage, vows, and the mandrake root ('love apples', R.V. margin), by which the attempt was made to attain this purpose (Gen. 30.14-17). But even the information we have is sufficient to make clear how dark a cloud lay over the spiritual life of many a woman. She was married, in order to bear offspring for her husband. 'Be fruitful, and multiply, and fill the earth' (Gen. 1.28). But what if the woman is unfruitful? It is only in recent times that it has become known that this deficiency may just as well be the responsibility of the husband as of the wife. Pliny was married three times, but had no children and was greatly distressed at it.[1] Did Pliny guess that he himself was the cause? He is more likely to have sought the cause in the three women, or in the hostility of the gods. From such facts as these we can realize that it is not just a form of words, but is really significant, when we find more than twenty times the statement: 'she conceived and bore'. The connection between intercourse and conception cannot simply be mathematically computed, and was certainly only recognized at a late date.

It is convenient to mention at this point, though it does not really belong here, that the actual births were clearly only rather casually concealed from public

---

[1] Poulsen, op. cit., p. 83.

HEALTH AND SICKNESS 51

view. For otherwise we should not so frequently find the image of the writhing and shrieking woman in travail.

> 'My body, my body, I am in travail,
> O walls of my heart, I cannot keep silence.'

How else should Jeremiah have acquired this picture? —Jeremiah, the most tender and yet most outspoken of the prophets (4.19 f.). Nor is it surprising to find that miscarriages play an important part. Jericho has water which prevents children from being born, or from living (one of the few Old Testament theories which, while hardly tenable, is at least not unnatural), until the prophet heals the spring, so that in the future the children will neither die nor be miscarried (II Kings 2.19-22). Job wishes that he had been a hidden, untimely birth (3.16); the Psalmist prays that his enemies may be as a miscarriage, which does not see the sun (58.8 [Heb. 9]). To the Preacher, the miscarriage is more fortunate than he who begets a hundred children (Eccl. 6.3); and Paul even uses the word ('one born out of due time') to describe himself (I Cor. 15.8). A miscarried child is called *nēphel*, which means literally a fall, or something fallen. But there is also a Hebrew word *něphīlīm*, obviously connected with it. This is usually translated 'giants' (Gen. 6.4, Num. 13.33, Ezek. 32.27 emended text). But in Ex. 21.22 (emended text) the same word means a miscarriage. We here get an indication of a popular belief which is unfortunately not elsewhere attested. From miscarriages, which are carefully buried, literally 'hidden' (Job 3.16), there went out evil spirits, which were no doubt thought to go about terrifying people and bringing disaster.[1] This too gives us a glimpse of the inner distresses which a Hebrew woman could suffer in childbirth. When Rachel died at the birth of her second son, she called him Ben-oni, that is 'son of the sinister power which is upon me'. His father changed the name to Ben-jamin, that is 'son of good fortune', Fortunatus (Gen. 35.18). A perineal rupture in childbirth is possibly indicated by the name Perez ('breach' Gen. 38.29).

Hebrew has formed a special type of word for the physically deformed and crippled. Of the three consonants of the word, the middle one is doubled, and the first syllable has the vowel i, and the second ē. Thus we find *'illēm*, dumb; *'iwwēr*, blind (in one eye or both); *gibbēaḥ*, bald-headed. The Assyro-Babylonian languages also have a special, though different, word-form. This in itself suggests that there were many deformed people, deaf, stammerers, dumb, blind, lame, paralysed, weak-sighted, hare-lipped, and many more. Further word-forms are also found to describe deformities and crippling. The lame man is vividly described 'The lame man's legs hang down—and so does the proverb in the mouth of fools' (Prov. 26.7, emended text). Remarkably enough, the left-handed person (whom the Greek Bible made into one who was ambidextrous), is described by a word for cripple, as the one who is hindered upon the right (Judg. 3.15, 20.16). Among 25,600 conscripted Benjaminites, there were seven hundred left-handers (Judg. 20.16). So if one were to go through the whole mass of the

---

[1] E. Samter, *Geburt, Hochzeit und Tod* (1911) shows how greatly in the Greek world everything connected with birth is surrounded by demons.

Hebrews, those who were afflicted in one way or another would be so numerous as hardly to be believed. The blind and those with serious eye afflictions were no doubt especially many in number. About 1930, the number of blind people in the world was estimated to be about 2,400,000. In China, there were five hundred to every hundred thousand people; in India one hundred and forty-two. In Egypt, in 1907, there were one thousand three hundred completely blind, and three thousand three hundred and twenty blind in one eye, a total of four thousand six hundred and fifty. In Poland the figure is one hundred in every hundred thousand, in Holland forty-six, in Belgium forty-four, in Switzerland (1910) sixty (with a total of two thousand four hundred blind persons). How many were there at any one time in ancient Palestine? Tobias was blinded by sparrow-dung (Tob. 2.10). Blinding is also mentioned (II Kings 25.7; Jer. 39.7). Nebuchadrezzar had King Zedekiah blinded; red-hot iron was placed close to the eye so that it lost its sight. But this was an isolated instance, and done by a foreigner, and its historicity has been questioned.

Many must have become cripples by breaking a bone; for while we hear of breaking bones, we do not hear of healing them (Lev. 21.19). Jonathan's five-year-old son was dropped by his nurse when they fled, and from that time on he was lame in his feet (II Sam. 4.4). It is true that the Hebrew has a word for doctor—rōphē', which originally meant 'mender, one who sews together', thus indicating one who tends wounds; but medical skill does not seem to have been very great. Job 13.4 speaks in derogatory fashion of 'medical

[1] Duhm, *Das Buch Jeremia* (1901), p. 278.

quacks'. Rather than go to such men, it was better to find other means, and so when his son Abijah was ill, King Jeroboam sent his wife to the prophet. She was to disguise herself so that the prophet should not know whose son was involved, but the prophet knew in spite of this (I Kings 14.1-6). Elijah the prophet, so we are told, sent a letter to King Jehoram: '. . . and thou shalt have great sickness by disease of thy bowels, until thy bowels fall out by reason of the sickness, day by day.' This happened after two years, 'and he died of sore diseases' (II Chron. 21.12-15). When Elisha came to Damascus, the sick King Benhadad called for his advice because of his illness (II Kings 8.7-9). Isaiah had a fig plaster put upon King Hezekiah, when he lay at the point of death, and he was healed (Isa. 38.1, 21 f.; 39.1). Ahaziah, injured by a fall, sent to Ekron to inquire concerning his suffering of the god Baal-Zebub there, and as a result incurred the censure of Elijah the prophet (II Kings 1.1-8). But the Syrian general Naaman himself journeyed to Elisha, on the advice which the Hebrew captive girl had given to his wife, to be cured of his skin disease (II Kings 5). Thus in addition to medical skill there is also the consulting of the god, or of men of God, and we are given a vivid description of how one such man healed a boy afflicted with sun or heat stroke (II Kings 4.18 ff.). After Elisha had been left alone with the sick child (cf. Mark 5.40), he prayed, and then 'he climbed upon the bed and lay upon the child, and put his mouth upon his mouth, and his eyes upon his eyes, and his hands upon his hands: and as he stretched himself upon him, the body of the child became warm. Then he got up, and walked to and fro in the house, and climbed up again and stretched himself over him, and the child sneezed seven times and opened his eyes.' In this, as in the case of David suffering from continual cold in his old age, we see the idea of the transference of life-force.

It is repeatedly stated that illness is a result of disobedience and sin. If Israel is obedient to God in Palestine, then it will have none of the illnesses which attacked it in Egypt. 'For,' we read, 'I Yahweh am your doctor' (Ex. 15.26). This statement must be quoted because a curious misunderstanding of it has produced practical consequences even down to the present day. There are even now Christians who adhere faithfully to the Bible who refuse, because of this statement, to have a doctor at all. They understand the phrase as if it meant: I, God alone, am your doctor. This would imply the rejection of all human doctors. In reality it implies a quite definite recognition of the doctor and his activities, for even God is described as a doctor.

As long as clear insight into the nature of a disease is lacking, its external features (symptoms) play an important part, however much they may happen to be merely a matter of chance and interchangeable. This is also true of the Hebrew. In the later period the significance of the cult, and particularly of the offering of the statutory sacrifices at the sanctuary, took on more and more importance, and also exerted an ever stronger influence upon the evaluation of the individual in everyday life. Anyone who does not take part in the cultus cannot be regarded as mature. For the Hebrew man, it is both duty and honour to be present at the cultic celebration. (Women were excluded from the public celebrations.) But in the cultus only those who are clean can take part, even though they may be only spectators. Cleanness is here not an aesthetic quality, but one which is partly moral and partly cultic. A man is clean who has no manifest guilt upon him, and especially no blood-guilt; one who is not disqualified by some sexual contact (I Sam. 21.5), or who is not suffering from certain diseases. By reason of this basic requirement, we are given in Lev. 13 a more detailed description of a skin disease which was clearly of common occurrence. Its symptoms are hardening, and spots on which the hair changes. The detail may be read in the passage itself. Whoever has these symptoms is pronounced unclean in the sense already described—and he is pronounced unclean not by the doctor, but by the priest. The sequel is, in the first place, a seven day separation (quarantine). The priest then undertakes a further examination and either pronounces the sick man clean from then on, that is, capable of taking part in the cult and of going about freely among his fellows, or pronounces him to be unclean, that is, not fit for the cult and needing to be kept separate.

The Hebrew calls this disease ṣāraʿat, which means 'stroke'. The meaning of this description is clearly that God has stricken the sick man, and has punished him thereby for sin. (We also use the word 'stroke' as the name of an illness, but for a quite different one.) As long as the illness lasts, the afflicted man must not merely live apart (cf. such sick men in II Kings 7.3 ff.), but must also wear torn garments, let his hair hang loose, cover his beard, and whenever he goes about in public, must cry 'Unclean, unclean'. This is to prevent anyone from coming near him unwittingly and catching the infection. For the same reason the lepers in the Middle Ages had to rattle little bits of wood as they went, and such wooden clappers were still used as toys in the childhood of some of us.

A short excursus into the New Testament is here appropriate. For in it those who suffer from the disease just described are called λεπροί, and this word is normally translated 'lepers'. We know that Jesus healed many such λεπροί. On one occasion (Luke 17.12-17) ten such sick men came to him, and he healed them all. He then commanded them to show themselves to the priests. This is exactly what is laid down in Lev. 13, and Jesus makes this order because only by the decision of the priest is it possible or permissible for the sick man to go about freely and 'clean' among his fellows. For as long as he is ill, he is not allowed to do so (Lev. 13.4 f., 21 ff.). Jesus healed these sick men and restored them to their community.[1] Now the disease described in Lev. 13 is certainly not the one which we call leprosy, but a skin disease (Vitiligo), and one which, as it is known, can be healed in a moment by a violent inner shock—in this case that experienced when the men, oppressed by their illness and their consequent separation from the community, are brought face to face with the holiness of Jesus. We should not therefore speak in the New Testament at all of leprosy and lepers, but of skin complaints and diseases. The same is true of the Old Testament, in Lev. 13, and in the case of Naaman the Syrian (II Kings 5).

[1] It has been thought possible to deduce from Jesus' instruction that he acknowledged the whole of the ceremonial law. But this assumption goes much too far. Jesus here acknowledges only a regulation made for reasons of public health. If he had not done this, those who had been healed by him would still have remained isolated from the community.

What we to-day call leprosy is quite different. This leprosy was once very prevalent in western Europe, but has now almost died out, apart from a small number of cases, for example in Norway and France, whereas in the East and in Africa thousands still suffer from it. For even now leprosy, except in its very earliest stages, is quite incurable. The sick man can only be avoided—which is unchristian—or cared for; he cannot be cured. The Old Testament also knows this disease, which might be called the most terrible of all diseases, but does not know of any specific name for it. The Job of the poem—though not of the prose framework—suffers from it, and, as far as his body is concerned, goes to his death without hope of deliverance. It is Bernhard Duhm to whom we owe the working out of this view, more than to anyone else.[1]

Plague, famine, wild beasts and war—these are the four great terrors of the earth, which the prophet knows, and which will come as judgment 'to cut off man and beast' (Ezek. 14.12 ff.). In the records there are preserved few clear comments on the nature of the plague, which still survives to-day in Asia, and formerly in Europe delivered up whole cities and countries to death. But Amos (6.9-11) sketches a picture of it with extreme vividness:

'And it shall come to pass, if there remain ten men in one house, that they shall die.
'And when a man's kinsman shall take him up, even he that burneth him, to bring out the bones out of the house, and shall say unto him that is in the innermost parts of the house, is there yet any with thee? and he shall say, No; then shall he say, Hold thy peace; mention not the

[1] *Das Buch Hiob* (1897).

name of the LORD. For behold, the LORD commandeth, and the great house shall be smitten into ruins, and the little house into pieces.'

(*d*) We may conclude this section with a few remarks by way of summary, for there is no particular value in lingering over odd details. Our sources give us no information concerning many diseases, nothing of infantile paralysis, the terror of present-day childhood, and nothing of cancer, the secret fear of many an ageing person to-day. That rheumatic complaints were not unknown to the Hebrew we have already seen from a discovery among the excavations. The variety of expressions for feverish complaints suggests tuberculosis and malaria, without being quite explicit about them. A lasting condition, and no doubt almost a universal one, is undernourishment, and the general weakening of strength and activity which it brings with it. Even to-day many millions live and die without ever having eaten until they were fully satisfied. Hunger and famine hang over the Hebrew like a dark cloud. It is partly aggravated by the lack of the means of communication to bring supplies where they are needed. We may recall Jacob, and Joseph and his brothers.

There is another point, a decisive one. Wherever to-day hunger and disease are prevalent, the spirit which is inspired by Jesus provokes the question: What can I, what can we all do about it? But this attitude is everywhere lacking where the light of the gospel has not yet called it forth. Finally there is the fact that wherever illness shows itself, the individual is driven out of the community. Not only must the mentally deranged Gerasene live far from his village among the graves (Mark 5.5)—that Jesus goes to him and speaks to him is an act of unprecedented compassion —and not only the man with skin-disease is separated as unclean (Lev. 13). Loneliness is the lot of every sick man. The thought that he is guilty; the idea that to belong to him, to be with him, is shameful and suggests guilt; the conviction that one is stricken by God because afflicted with suffering—all this must be borne in mind, and its nature felt, if we are to get a real picture of the health and sickness of the Hebrew.

We turn now to the course of the Hebrew's life.

4

HOW THE HEBREW LIVED I

WE may begin with a note on the question of maturity. As we have seen, Num. 14.29 and 32.11 assume that Hebrew men aged twenty already have sons. A Hebrew—we may call him Joel—marries at the age of eighteen, and when he is nineteen, he has a son called Abner. This Abner, like his father, also marries at eighteen and has his first son at nineteen, whom we may call Eli. Thus Joel is a father at nineteen, and a grandfather at thirty-eight. If Eli does the same as his father and grandfather, and his first son is called Machir, then, when Machir is one year old, his father Eli is twenty, his grandfather Abner is thirty-nine, and his great-grandfather Joel is fifty-eight. Every one of these assumptions is well within the bounds of possibility.

What this means only becomes clear when we make a modern comparison. A young man to-day, whom we may call Paul, marries at twenty-five, which under modern conditions is probably rather early. When Paul is twenty-six, his first son Fred is born. Fred's first son Ernest, under the same assumptions, will come into the world when his grandfather Paul is fifty-two. Ernest's first son, John, will likewise be born when Paul, his great-grandfather, is seventy-eight. When John is one year old, his father Ernest will be twenty-seven, his grandfather Fred fifty-three, and his great-grandfather Paul seventy-nine. This gives us the following comparison:

Father: Hebrew at nineteen, to-day at twenty-six.
Grandfather: Hebrew at thirty-eight, to-day at fifty-two.
Great-grandfather: Hebrew at fifty-seven, to-day at seventy-eight.

As a rule women marry and become mothers two to three years earlier than men marry and become fathers. Thus we get the following comparison:

Mother: Hebrew at sixteen, to-day at twenty-four.
Grandmother: Hebrew at thirty-five, to-day at forty-nine.
Great-grandmother: Hebrew at fifty-four, to-day at seventy-five.

A number of considerations follow from these figures. One of these will be discussed when we deal with marriage laws. A second consideration is that the expectation of becoming a great-grandparent is much smaller for the modern than for the Hebrew. We may recall the words of the Decalogue: 'to the third and fourth generation' (Ex. 20.5), which clearly includes great-grandparents. A third consideration is that the earlier time of marriage among the Hebrews deprives the growing youth of those years of freedom and mobility, of broader education and of travel abroad, whose values we should not like to see lost to the life of our young people.

But there is another consideration which very much

concerns us. A man takes a wife, enjoys her love, awaits the first child with her, experiences its birth, and then feels his responsibility as a father; he watches the child grow from a baby in arms to the child at play, to the schoolboy, the youth, and the independent person, and then sees his own child have children of his own and so is called grandfather. In all this, he goes through a process of maturing of the greatest significance. He may welcome it and be aware of it, or not; he may be sensitive and thoughtful, or thoughtless and lacking in feeling, but he experiences this maturing, which goes on quietly and unobserved. We may overlook this process, but, if we are aware of it, we cannot overestimate its importance. Now this maturity was reached, as we have seen from the figures, much earlier among the Hebrews than it is to-day, and, in spite of the Hebrew's shorter expectation of life, it was more generally reached than to-day. Perhaps we may, at least in part, explain from this the leaning of the Hebrew, as of the ancients in general, towards wisdom. The Hebrew was more experienced in life, and therefore also wiser in life. And in this connection we may also note that, when it is said of Jesus that he was 'about thirty years old' at his first public appearance (Luke 3.23), this note places him on a par with our men of forty, rather than with our thirty-year-olds. Jesus kept silence up to this age.

The first experience which a new-born Hebrew underwent was that he was given a name, sometimes by his father, sometimes by his mother.[1] We know about one thousand four hundred names from the Old

---

[1] The Old Testament mentions forty-six cases of naming, twenty-eight times by the mother, eighteen times by the father.

Testament, and, so far as we may judge, about two thousand four hundred individuals. Concerning most of these, we know little more than their names. Much could be said about these names, but only a short survey is here possible.[1] We learn, for example, concerning the sons of Jacob (Gen. 29 and 30), why they were given the names they bore. The interpretations are often of a popular kind, and the real meaning of the name is a different one. But be that as it may, it is the prevailing view among the Hebrews that names have meaning, they 'speak'. Only at a late date, from about 400 B.C. onwards, do we find the custom of choosing a traditional name, because of someone formerly called by it, rather than because of its meaning. Even then, it was never the name of the father that was chosen for the son, but at the most that of the grandfather, and even then probably only if the grandfather was already dead.[2] From Jesse, the father of David, right down to the last king of Judah, runs a line of twenty-two names; no two of them are the same. We find further, that a man may change his name: Abram become Abraham, Gideon Jerubbaal, Mattaniah was renamed Zedekiah by the king of Babylon (II Kings 24.17).

More than half the surviving names are theophoric.

[1] The very good study by Martin Noth, *Die israelitischen Personennamen im Rahmen der gemeinsemitischen Namengebung* (1928) deserves to be reissued with account taken of new material.

[2] So-called 'papponymy'. The view is that in the grandson the deceased grandfather comes to life again. The German word for grandson, 'Enkel', is derived from 'eninchili'—'little grandfather'. The same view, that the deceased father or grandfather appears in the new-born child, underlies the Greek names, Ἀντίπατρος, Ἀντίπαππος, which are both shortened to Ἀντιπᾶς, and Thomas (twin) is originally only the name for a boy whose older brother has died shortly before. Barabbas—'son of the father'—also derives from the same idea. Similarly Seth in Gen. 4.25 (where the statement is made explicitly) and Tahath (I Chron. 6.24, Heb. 9) both mean 'substitute', and Shobab (II Sam. 5.14, I Chron. 2.18) means 'return, substitute'.

They consist of two parts, of which either the first or the second is the name or the designation of a deity. Thus Nathaniah means 'Yahweh has given'. If the first part contains the name or designation of the deity, there is a special emphasis upon this.[1] Thus Jonathan means 'It is Yahweh (and no other god) who has given', and Elnathan means 'It is the godhead (and no one else) who has given'. All these four names may be shortened by the omission of the theophoric part, and thus we get Nathan ('he has given'). There are many such abbreviated forms, called 'short names', and for the most part we are not in a position to say from what full names they have been abbreviated. Besides these theophoric names, there are many which ask some quality for the bearer. Tamar probably means: 'may you be as beautiful as a palm-tree'; Tirzah means 'well-pleasing'; Azzan 'strong'; Delilah 'little one' (rather like 'darling'), Peninnah 'with thick hair', Basemath 'smelling of ointment', Shobek 'pre-eminent'. There are many of these names, with which the parents desired to keep always present a wish for the nature or the fortune of their child.

By contrast, we find a group of names of the opposite kind, designed, namely, to have the effect of a talisman. There hovers over the life of the child the fear of what might come upon it, and this is expressed in a name which says what the child should not be. Thus Gareb means 'scabious', Kelita 'dwarf', Zeruiah 'afflicted with skin-disease', Nabal 'fool' (which is equivalent to 'godless'), concerning whom his prudent wife says, at the moment when David's vengeance is

[1] L. Köhler, 'Syntax zweier hebräischer Namengruppen', *Vetus Testamentum*, II, pp. 374-377.

about to fall upon him: 'As his name is, so is he; Nabal is his name, and folly (*nĕbālā*) is with him' (I Sam. 25.25).

Two more groups of names deserve mention. The one consists of protective names. The Bedouin say that they give to their slaves beautiful, virtuous names, like 'good, faithful, honourable', their slaves being meant to behave towards them in the manner implied by their names. But to their children they give names full of threatening and resistance, for their children are to be as their names suggest, full of threats, defiance, challenge, resistance against their enemies.[1] Exactly in the same way we find among the Hebrews the names Caleb, that is, 'one who bites like a dog', Nun and Nahash, 'the eel' and 'the snake'; Zeeb 'the wolf', Simeon 'the hyaena-dog', Parosh 'the flea'—a name still much used among the Semites (for the louse is regarded throughout the east as friendly and bearable, but the flea as uncongenial and as an unbearable pest). There are other such names.

There is a last group, not much discussed until recently—the occasional names. When, during the 'Battle of the Nations' at Leipzig, the wife of the priest in a nearby village bore twin daughters, their father called them Kanonina and Bombardina. A Swiss, already father of four daughters, but having no son, called his fifth child—another daughter —simply Quinta (fifth). A Ruala, Hamar-abu-Amrad, struck his pregnant wife, and this annoyed her. She therefore called the son who was born shortly

---

[1] J. J. Hess, *Von den Beduinen des Innern Arabiens* (1938), p. 1381: 'We name our sons for our enemies, but our slaves for ourselves.' This statement is traced by Hess as far back as Ibn Doreid (d. 933).

afterwards Zaʻal 'annoyance'. These are occasional names. It is naturally difficult, when we do not know the circumstances, to get the sense of such occasional names. But here must belong such names as Nogah 'ray of light' (born at early dawn); Barak 'lightning' (born during a storm); Geshem 'rain'; Mahol 'processional dance' (born at the time of the dance); Zebah 'sacrifice' (born at the time of the sacrifice); Zerah 'sunrise'; Hodesh 'new-moon'; Hathath 'confusion'; Harhur 'fever-heat' (possibly born while the mother had fever); Manoah 'resting-place' (born at the resting-place); Matri 'born during rain'; Beera, Beeri (born at the well); Hothir 'he leaves over' (where all the rest have died); Gahar 'rainless time'; and many more. Quite clear are such names as Haggi, Haggith, and Haggai, which all three mean 'born on the festival day', and Shabbethai 'born on the Sabbath'. Exactly similar is the Syriac Bardeḥadbeshabba 'born on the first day of the week (Sunday)', and the Latin Dominicus, 'born on the day of the Lord', which has survived in the Swiss surnames Nigg, Mink and Meng, and in the Romansh girls' name Menga. If we knew the exact circumstances of the naming in the case of all the Hebrew occasional names, we should have a lively picture of the individual life of the Hebrew.[1]

When the child, thus individualized by the giving of a name, grows up and enters into the communal

[1] Occasional names in Tigrai (N. Abyssinia): *'Atgawha* 'he came at day-break', *Zalamtani* (Arabic) 'thou hast done me wrong', and *'Eggub* 'one who did wrong'. Names, given by a mother who dies in childbirth, cf. Littmann, *Aksum*, IV, pp. 58, 65. Occasional names among the Tonga people (south of Mozambique): *Ndleleni* '(born) on the way'; *Nkuweni* 'under the fig-tree'; *Humbini* 'at the time of the locusts'; *Nyimpini* 'during the war'; *Nualungna* 'son of the north' (born when a strong north wind was blowing): cf. *Schweizer Mission in Südafrika*, No. 114 (1945), pp. 104 f.

life, and particularly when it is his lot to distinguish himself in public life and so to be often named, an addition is made to his individual name, as among us the family name is added to the first name or Christian name—Bethuel, son of Nahor; Kish, father of Saul; Benjamin, brother of Joseph; Ephron the Hittite; Jesse the Bethlehemite; Helez the Paltite; Goliath of Gath; Eli the priest; and so forth. But these personal particulars[1] already place the Hebrew in his community, and need not concern us here further.

The Hebrew infant belongs to the mother, and is nursed by her. Only rarely does a nurse take the mother's place. We may recall Moses, who was taken from his mother at the age of three months and by a stratagem had his own mother as nurse (Ex. 2.3-9). Such nurses were held in high honour, as we can see from the mention of the burial of Deborah, the nurse of Rebecca (Gen. 35.8). The time during which a child is breast-fed—especially if it is the first, or only child—is unusually long, being up to three or four years. At any rate Hannah took her son Samuel, as soon as she had weaned him, to be an attendant to the priest at the sanctuary at Shiloh, and he could already perform small duties (I Sam. 1.21 ff.; 2.18). Weaning was the occasion for a banquet, at least for the well-to-do (Gen. 21.8). Even after this the girls remain in the sphere of the mother and of the other women of the household, but the boys gradually move out of that circle, and follow the father and the other male members of the household, watch all their activities, learn them, and are soon employed in all manner of duties and services.

[1] L. Köhler, ' Die Personalien des Oktateuch ', Z.A.W. 40 (1922), pp. 20-36.

The same thing can still be seen to-day in the families of the smaller peasants and artisans. The Hebrew knows nothing of childhood as a time of play and indulgence.

This is a suitable point at which to say a word concerning the density of population amid which the Hebrew grew up. For the development of a man is much dependent upon this. Men grow and develop differently, whether in the monotonous loneliness of the great city, in the cloistered quiet of the farmstead, or in the friendly intimacy of the small village. The Hebrew grew up in a peasant village. Even the well-known towns like Jerusalem and Samaria, apart from the royal seat and the court and court-temple formed on foreign pattern, and its attendant population of officials and staff, were just large peasant villages. Isaiah can express the judgment of God to Jerusalemites and Judahites with the picture of the vinetender (Isa. 5.1-7). The greeting: 'Yahweh himself keep thy going out and thy coming in', where going out in the morning to work in the fields is placed before coming in from the fields towards evening (Ps. 121.8), applies equally to the town. It was not only the hill-dweller Amos from the highlands of Judah, but also the prophets who worked in the towns, who all use similes from the tending of cattle, from the world of plants, from farming activities, and are understood. The whole of Palestine, with all its settlements, was just a land of peasants, and its inhabitants almost all engaged in farming.

There are strict laws governing the development of the peasant village. Its inhabitants live from the produce of the land within the boundary. If their number increases, the boundary must extend. If it extends, it will soon become so large that the outermost stretches of land lie too far out for cultivation, since the journey to and from the fields takes up too much time. When this happens there is nothing else to be done but for part of the population to move out and found a daughter-village. The book of Joshua speaks of many such 'daughters' of villages.[1] We may make a rough guess that a Hebrew village did not contain more than about three to five hundred inhabitants. Nearby are much smaller settlements, which may be described as farmsteads ($ḥāẓēr$). These are hamlets in which probably one individual with his family, his relatives, slaves and dependents originally settled. Even the larger settlements, and Jerusalem itself, will hardly have contained more than a few thousand inhabitants. They are moreover divided into quarters: Upper City, Lower City, Old City, New City. This is explicitly stated for Hebron in its other name Kiriath 'Arba' 'town of the four (quarters)'. The separate quarters probably did not have much to do with one another.

The Hebrew thus grew up in a fairly small community, in which everyone knows everyone else, observes, judges, has contact in friendship or hostility. One is never alone. One does what everybody else does. One sees what everyone else does. To this is added the fact that the whole of daily life takes place in the open air, in that space between the houses which we call the street, although there were no real streets, but only the irregularly shaped pieces of ground on which no houses stand. The house itself, very simple and without

[1] A study of place names and positions of places from the point of view of settlement-policy would be valuable.

light—the woman in the parable of the lost coin had to light her lamp to search for what she had lost (Luke 15.8)—serves only as a sleeping place at night, and as protection in time of rain. As far as possible, men live in the open air. We need a reason for leaving the house; the Hebrew needs a reason for going into it. The child thus grows up in the street, among the adults, watches their affairs, assists in them as soon as he can, as much as he is able, or imitates them in play. He listens to conversations, to laughter, to cares, to gossip and quarrels. Nothing is strange to him or hidden from him. With his large eyes foreboding and dreaming, he looks ahead to the days when he too will be grown up, and he knows only a small part of that innocence, that lack of anxiety about the future, that playfulness and childlike quality, which the modern child knows.

Very soon some work falls upon him. He looks after his younger brothers and sisters, he carries things to his mother, he collects manure to burn on the hearth, he watches over the smaller domestic animals, he helps in the pasture, in the field, he does what he sees father and mother doing. Even in early youth he already stands between the life of childhood and that of the adults, drawn into the divisions of households and neighbourhoods. It occurs to no one to think that there are things which he is still to young to see, or to speak of, or to take part in. We could speak more seriously of an overburdening of the Hebrew youth, were it not that the amount of work done by the Hebrew is much smaller than what modern man can and must do on the average—partly because of the simplicity of his existence, and partly because of the limit set to his strength by undernourishment and variations of nourishment. For plenty and famine, satiety and hunger, must always have alternated rapidly and violently, since the possibility of accumulating supplies for a longer period and of keeping them eatable was so slight. But the daily work, which begins with the first light of day, is soon ended, long before the evening darkness falls rapidly, with only a short period of twilight. The working day is not long, and around midday, the whole land is at rest.[1]

We hear little of children at play. Herodotus tells us that during a famine the Lydians invented the game of dice, and bones and ball, in order to distract their attention from the gnawing pain in their stomachs (1.94). These games are to be found throughout the world and appear everywhere in the earliest times, just as everywhere children light upon the idea of discerning human and animal forms in stones and pieces of wood, and imitate with them in play the activity of men and animals. This must also have happened among the Hebrews, and there will have been cries and songs to accompany it. But no trace of it has remained. The only thing that is said is that in the day of the fulfilment of salvation the open places of Jerusalem will be filled with boys and girls at play (Zech. 8.5). On the day after Jesus' entry into Jerusalem the children imitated this entry in play, to the annoyance of the priests (Matt. 21.15), and no doubt the forty-two boys

[1] L. Köhler, 'Der Tageslauf des Hebräers', *Protestantische Monatshefte* (1921), pp. 233 ff. The variation from a day and night both of twelve hours amounts to three hours forty-seven minutes in Zürich, but in Palestine only two hours eight minutes. Thus the longest day there is one hour thirty-nine minutes shorter than in Zürich, and the shortest day the same amount longer. The days lengthen and shorten more slowly than in Zürich, the twilight is shorter, the fall of night and the day-break more sudden. For places further north than Zürich, the difference is all the greater.

of Bethel who followed Elisha calling out: 'Go up, thou bald-head' only meant it as a harmless game (II Kings 2.23 ff.).

Herodotus also reports that among the Persians the boys were not seen by their fathers until they were five years old, in order that—so the rationalizing Greek historian adds—the father need not be troubled if the boy dies during the period of nursing (1.136). Meribaal, the grandson of Saul, was also five years old when his nurse let him fall so that he was lame from then on (II Sam. 4.4). In the time of Nehemiah, Jews had married women from Ashdod, Ammon and Moab; but their children could not speak 'in the Jews' language' at all (Neh. 13.24). How little we may speak of a proper, deliberate education by the mother such as we normally think of to-day, may be seen from the 'praise of the virtuous woman' (Prov. 31.10-31). She is active on behalf of her house and family day and night. She has the confidence of her husband. She looks after the food and provisions and the increase of possessions. She cares for the poor. She is proud of the position of her husband. She speaks sensibly, and guides them all with wise direction. Her sons bless her, and her daughters honour her. Her fear of God is without fail. But that she educates her children is not mentioned at all. Education takes place naturally, without any deliberate purpose. It is achieved by example and pattern, but as a subject of discussion and consideration it is unknown.

The education of the growing youth rests entirely upon the father. The fact that Hannah, with her husband's agreement, dedicates her son to the sanctuary, happens because of her vow. Otherwise the son grows up into the trade, or, if one may so call it, the profession of his father. In the case of boys born to a man by a slave, who have grown up entirely among the free-born, it is the father's will which is decisive. But this does not make much difference, since trades and professions are little differentiated. Only at a later time do we hear anything of real industries, and even these, like all real crafts down to our own time, are handed down within the family. The priesthood is strictly limited to inheritance. Micah, in the mountain country of Ephraim, who made for himself a sanctuary with the necessary vessels, committed the priesthood to one of his sons, but removed it from him as soon as he gained possession of a Levite who had from his fathers the right to be a priest (Judg. 17). It is explicitly stated of Jeremiah that he belonged to the priests who lived in Anathoth in the land of Benjamin (1.1). There was no sanctuary in Anathoth, but Abiathar the priest had been banished thither (I Kings 2.26 f.), and with him his family, the descendants of Eli, the priest at the time-honoured sanctuary of Shiloh. We are probably not wrong in finding in Jeremiah's words on Jerusalem something also of the superiority of a formerly honoured priesthood over the newcomers of the Solomonic sanctuary. Priestly nobility is perhaps the only nobility the Hebrews knew. The royal houses and their pretensions (Zeph. 1.8) are half outside the community of the people. Even Solomon was all too prone to foreign influences of various kinds.

Together with actual work and methods of executing it, the son also learnt from his father a wealth of practical wisdom; the assessing of cattle and of soil, the judgment of the weather, the choice of a favourable time for the duties of the annual cycle, the measuring of time, no doubt at first by the position of the sun and the length of shadows, the many signs and omens, derived from sound ancient observation of the connections of events, or taken over from all manner of superstition. Neither work in the fields, nor the rearing, the bartering, buying and selling of cattle, nor the building of a house, nor the exchange of goods can be carried on entirely without counting, measuring and weighing. So the son learns from his father a simple standard of numbers and sizes and their relationship. Calculation is the basis of common life and work. The common Semitic word for reckoning (ḥāshab) originally meant to cut, to notch, for elsewhere too there is generally known the custom of marking things with notches, or scratches, and then to calculate with them—laboriously, but reliably—to manage one's affairs, and so far as is necessary, to trade.

How about writing and reading? Two different things must here be distinguished—the reading and writing of marks, signs and notches, and the reading and writing of an alphabet. It was an ancient custom to mark one's cattle, one's implements and such like with a stroke, a circle, or a combination of strokes, circles and points, in short with a sign which ranks as the property of a family or a clan, and was recognized, so as to protect from theft. These signs were known, in so far as they were customary in one's own tribe or village, and they were readily distinguishable.[1] That was the oldest form of reading. The son learned this

---

[1] 'Here is my signature (margin 'mark'), let the Almighty answer me.' So Job closes his complaint (31.35). (cf. p. 160 n. 1).

from his father. It is a more difficult matter to put these marks on for oneself. Perhaps there were only a few people in any one place who were capable of this, and the rest utilized their services. These were the oldest scribes, indispensable and held in high honour. No doubt they also always possessed a larger or smaller fund of knowledge concerning various practices, customs and rights. All law is in origin the law of custom, and new laws of custom are always being formed, while old laws fall out of use and cease to be valid.

A script in the proper sense, that is a series of signs by the aid of which words and phrases and sentences can be built up without risk of misunderstanding, was not invented or developed by the Hebrews themselves, any more than by the majority of modern peoples. What they possessed and used by way of script was borrowed. We do not know from whence they derived it. We do not know how far the art of reading and writing it was spread among them. The art of reading was certainly more general than that of writing. The centre of both arts will have been the royal courts, the households of great lords (in so far as there were any such), and the sanctuaries. Perhaps there were also in every period travelling specialists, uprooted from normal life, who were qualified in this art, travelled through the land and, wherever they were needed, were pleased to exercise their skill and so eke out a living. But what we think of as school and schooling was alien to the Hebrew even until the latest period. Even Jeremiah needed Baruch, a professional scribe, to write down his words. The fact that kings had writings and messages read out to them is not merely a sign of their honourable position, but is also a matter of lack of schooling. Messages go rather by word of mouth. And this lack of schools is accompanied by the absence of another great power—there is no training in the orderly use of time. Without schooling, such regular usage cannot exist, and it is lacking to the Hebrew. He is no slave of time. Time does not control him; he controls it and uses it and spends it as seems right to him.

Where schools are lacking, schooling need not be absent. The Hebrew had to teach his son many things, and what the brother learned, the sister might learn with him. There was the question of how to greet an acquaintance or a stranger, an old man, and one of higher rank, or one of equal age and one of lower rank; how to receive and answer a greeting; how to put a question, how to make a request, give information, grant or reject a wish. All this had to be learnt, for life together, and dealings in the street, on the open place before the gate, in the field and the pasture have their proper fixed forms, handed down from very ancient times.[1] Everyone addressed everyone else as 'thou'—old and young, men and women, masters and slaves, king and warrior, priest and prophet. But the finer distinctions were by no means lacking, and they have their proper meaning. There were the unwritten laws of a conversation, unwritten but also unbreakable; you could not break them and escape the consequences.[2] Even to-day one may hear real peasant folk engaging in a long conversation which consists entirely in formalities. None is out of place, none is omitted, none is lacking in meaning and appositeneses, none is irrele-

---

[1] L. Köhler, 'Hebräische Gesprächsformen', Z.A.W. 40 (1922), pp. 36 ff.
[2] Irene Lande, *Formelhafte Wendungen der Umgangssprache im Alten Testament* (Leiden, 1949).

vant, none betrays the personal mannerisms of the speaker, none betrays what a person does not wish to say, none remains without proper sense and full weight to the one who understands it. There is no lack of hidden cunning in the words, no lack of agreeing to a promise, or refusing one, or disclosing one, no lack of ambiguity in a threat, or of many other such nuances. The whole may well appear to a stranger, unfamiliar with it, as a mere play of commonplace remarks, even of phrases without any meaning. But those who are in the know are aware of what is meant, and for them neither the goal of the discussion, nor the way it is going, nor its result, is unclear. Wherever men live closely together, where the daily round, and all the relationships and concerns of life are closely and in manifold fashion interwoven, the word, the right word in the right place, is well known, and practised. The delicate allusion, the casual excuse, the apparently chance, purposeless silence, all speak with a clear language. The fact that the young David was called *něbōn dābār*—skilled in word (I Sam. 16.18)—had more weight than we suspect, and it represents high praise for his father Jesse to whom he owes this faculty. Everywhere in the Old Testament in questions and answers and conversations, we find this assurance of forms and expressions, and this skill in natural speech; this is not literature, but the reflection of actual life. If we visualize the skilful use of words with which Abigail encountered the wounded pride of David—no woman, and indeed no man, could have spoken more eloquently—or the defiant insolence of Jezebel, the king's daughter, or Naomi's answer to the greetings of the people of Bethlehem, or the wisdom of the woman of Tekoa before David, and so many more like these, we become aware that the daughters did not lag behind the sons when their fathers trained their children in the art of right speech.

It hardly needs to be added that training also covered the practical aspects of life. It dealt with the rights which belonged to each man as regards pieces of land, pastures, inheritances and such like. It concerned the rites, the abstentions and actions which accompanied sacrificial festivals; participation in the covenant community; the sentences, customs and traditions in cases of disagreement, and their adjustment, and those appropriate to misdemeanours and crimes and their atonement; the ordering and controlling of public affairs, so far as such existed. In short, it covered every conceivable aspect and manifestation of common life. Concerning the details of all this, we know next to nothing.

Training in questions of belief, and the honouring of the deity, was also the affair of the father and of the elders. The sacred places and times, which must be attended to with caution and with the observance of definite, strict rules, provided the occasion for the boy to ask 'Why?' 'Whence?' and 'To what purpose?' The answer is the father's business. 'When your sons say to you, What is this sacred custom, which you observe? you are to say, It is the sacrifice of Yahweh's Passover, for . . .' (Ex. 12.26 ff.). The devout Jew observes this prescription for the Passover to-day. Moreover, in the fifth book of Moses the Hebrew was repeatedly enjoined to instruct his children and to throw light on matters for them: 'Thou shalt make them known to thy sons and to thy sons' sons' (Deut.

4.9). 'Thou shalt teach them repeatedly to thy sons, and shalt talk of them when thou sittest in thine house, and when thou walkest by the way, and when thou liest down, and when thou risest up' (6.7). 'When thy son asketh thee in time to come, saying, What mean the testimonies, and the statutes, and the judgments, which Yahweh our God hath commanded you? then thou shalt say unto thy son . . .' (6.20 f.). 'And ye shall teach them your children, talking of them . . .' (11.19). Even if these commands belong only to the seventh century, their setting and their essential content is centuries older.

Occasions for such questions and such instruction arose every day. In the common pasture stands a boundary-stone: why is it there? On the border of the property stands out a group of sacred trees: why are they sacred? At a certain time, it is proper to go to the sanctuary and hold a sacrificial meal: why is this done? On certain days, it is not permitted to eat food: why not? The whole of life is accompanied, restricted, regulated by observances, customs, prohibitions, festivals and recitals. There is an abundance of occasions for children to ask questions and seek information. Not every father will always have been able to satisfy them. But there were old men, wise, knowing men, priests, story-tellers, and their words fell upon attentive ears. So from generation to generation the tradition and the instruction were passed on in living form. What man would not be proud to be able to give information? In such ways the material of the Old Testament has to a large extent been brought together.

It is somewhat like this that we must picture the training of the younger generation of Hebrews—

without books, or schoolrooms, but by word of mouth. In such training, however, there lies concealed something which must not be overlooked. It provides a great deal of real education. Recognition of traditions handed down from the distant past gives consciousness of one's own special place; descent from ancestors, with whom God has done great things, gives a feeling of nobility. Heroes awaken a longing for imitation; virtues awaken noble resolutions; adventures form a picture of life and shape one's conception of one's own life. Each man, and particularly the simple man, such as the Hebrew is for the most part, understands his own experience, how it comes upon him and how he himself actively shapes it, in the light of the conceptions and the picture which he has absorbed into himself from the life-experience of others.

Here we may point to a thread which runs through all the great Hebrew stories. For it admits of no possible doubt that these stories, whether in the form in which they have become part of the Old Testament tradition or in other forms deviating to a greater or less extent from this, have worked formatively, moulding the conceptions, the expectations and the ideals of men. We should not indeed have these stories at all had they not been told and re-told through a whole series of generations until they were written down. Their materials are centuries old, with the exception of the later examples, like the life of Jeremiah or the deeds of Nehemiah. They were also related after the time of their writing down, and side by side with it. For who could read them? How could they possibly be spread abroad among the people in a large number of copies? Reading and copying were only possible to a limited extent. They were read aloud, and they were recited in whole or in part exactly as one may even to-day find reciters, often simple shepherds, reciting Dante's *Divina Commedia* in separate cantos to the people, in front of St. Mark's in Florence or in the Abruzzi mountains. There thus appear reciters at the great pilgrim festivals at the sanctuaries, who recited to the Hebrew people old and new stories between the sacrifices and cultic observances.

Now all these stories, whether they tell of Abraham or Joseph or Moses or Saul or David, have one basic feature in common. They tell of the mutability of human fortunes, and the immutability of the faithfulness of God. There is Joseph, for example, the spoilt son, born late to an aged father and his favourite wife. He makes himself hated by his brothers by his high-flown dreams. They try to kill him, but he escapes. He is hawked about as a slave and comes to be overseer in his master's house. When he is put in prison, he shows kindness to his fellow prisoners and is forgotten by them. He becomes the saviour of Pharaoh and of his people, a deliverer for his fathers and brothers and their household and for the patriarchs of the people. There is Moses; before his birth he was threatened with death, cherished by his loving mother, exposed and saved. He became a murderer and had to flee the land, was called to be deliverer of his people, and by his people was insulted, threatened, burdened with all manner of discouraging toil, but lived on in full powers to extreme age. He died alone, and was buried not by his people but by God, so that none knows where his grave is to be found. There is David, the shepherd boy, the harpist to the king, the hero and son-in-law of Saul, threatened with murder, a fugitive from the land, leader of a band and freebooter, founder of the state, lord over a people and a land, and lord far beyond its boundaries. His first child by Bathsheba dies in spite of his fasting; his son Amnon is slain by his son Absalom, his son Absalom is slain by his sister's son Joab; 70,000 of his people were struck down by plague; in his old age he was powerless and helpless in the struggles for the succession. How much of glory and how much of misery! One cannot follow these and many other life-histories without becoming aware that no man knows to what heights life may raise him, or to what depths it may fling him down. None can see the way ahead, and none can shape it for himself. The only way of life is to wait and keep silence. For, as it runs in the Song of Hannah:

> 'Yahweh killeth, and maketh alive,
> He bringeth down to the grave, and bringeth up.
> Yahweh maketh poor and maketh rich:
> He bringeth low, he also lifteth up.' (I Sam. 2.6 f.)

These thoughts, this same picture of life, has come through the Song of Mary (Luke 1.52 f.) into our own liturgies, and still lives and shapes our conception of life, as for example in the words of the hymn:

> 'All are alike before His face;
>   'Tis easy to our God most High
> To make the rich man poor and base,
>   To give the poor man wealth and joy.
> True wonders still by Him are wrought,
> Who setteth up, and brings to nought.'[1]

[1] Georg Neumark, trans. Catherine Winkworth, *Lyra Germanica* I (1855), p. 153.

These thoughts, these conceptions, this picture of life and these expectations of what may come, do not provoke to action and do not spur men on to bold new undertakings, and yet do not work to stultify and to enjoin inactivity, but lead along a middle path to calmness and composure from day to day. With this we may end our comments on the training and education of the young Hebrew lad.

But we have not yet spoken of the female children. There is not much to say. Whereas the boy, from about the age of five years, left the circle of his mother and lived more and more in his father's sphere of life, in his company, in imitation of his activity, assisting in his father's work, the girl remained with her mother and the other female members of the household. Her whole life through the Hebrew woman stood under the guardianship of a man, at first that of her father, and then that of her husband. If father and husband died, the nearest and oldest male relation, grandfather or brother or brother-in-law on the husband's side, took over, but even where these were lacking, the eldest son, as soon as he was grown, took over the tutelage of the woman. This is the real bitterness which makes the woman once called Naomi wish to be called Mara (Ruth 1.20). She has lost husband and sons, and has no grandsons. She has no man in the circle of her relationship near enough for her to depend upon his guardianship, 'for the Almighty has brought bitter things (*mar*) upon me'. Here again the marvellous and joyous part of her experience is that she can lay a son of Ruth's in her bosom,[1] and her neighbours can say 'A son is

[1] L. Köhler. 'Die Adoptionsform von Ruth 4.16', Z.A.W. 29 (1909), pp. 312 ff.

born to Naomi' (4.17). Thus she becomes the ancestress of David, and no longer lives in a family circle denuded of men.

The extent to which the Hebrew woman was restricted by the guardianship of the man is not easy to determine. There was no lack of women who acted independently: Rebecca, Deborah, Jael, Abigail, and a whole series of such characters. There may be legal restraint, and yet in daily life complete freedom of action; on all sides we see the Hebrew woman enjoying this freedom. But there were nevertheless two worlds, that of the man and that of the woman. Custom held them apart from each other, and the Hebrew girl grew up in this remoteness from male activity, at the mother's side, in her company, in service and learning with her, in her conversation, from which the girl early learned to understand the proper sphere and position of woman.

5

HOW THE HEBREW LIVED II

WHEN Abraham was ninety-nine years old, circumcision was made obligatory for him as a sign of the covenant between God and himself (Gen. 17). This narrative is late, but it does not lack ancient elements. To these ancient elements belongs no doubt the statement that when Abraham carried out circumcision on himself and on Ishmael, the son of Hagar, and on all the male members of his household, Ishmael was just thirteen years old (17.25), and this is still the age at which the devout Jew becomes responsible under the law (*bar miṣwāh*). It is the age at which the boy becomes a man. Physical maturity came earlier for the Hebrew, as for all southern peoples, for the female sex as much as two or three years earlier, and with physical maturity the Hebrew ranked as adult. The time of childhood was past, the time of responsibility had arrived, even if, where the parents were wise, entry upon it might be delayed a little longer.

The Hebrew man, for so we must now describe the still by no means fully-grown youth, entered four great communities: he was ready to take his share in religious practice, in marriage, in law, and in warfare. For each of these four capacities meant the entry into a great community; that of those who offer sacrifice, of those who are married, of those who administer law, and of the warriors. The full nature of this, and all that it brings with it, can only be worked out in a study of the Hebrew community. Here only those aspects are mentioned which affected the individual.

The importance which the priestly narrative gives to the sacrifices by the priesthood at the central sanctuary makes us miss only too easily the part which every Hebrew man played in sacrifice. The greater sacrificial festivals will always have begun by subjecting those who took part to a confession—that is an establishing of their fitness and worthiness for taking part in the cultus. When David in Nob asked for food for his men from the priest Ahimelech, the priest first established the cultic cleanness of the hungry men, since he only had sanctified bread (I Sam. 21.5 f.). Evidence of this kind was necessary before every cultic action. We may turn the words of the decalogue into questions in the form: 'Have you not . . . ?', 'Hast thou not . . . ?'. A type of confessional questioning of this kind, transferred to a higher level, may be derived from Ps. 15. Thus we can get a picture of the kind of examination of fitness for the cultus which the Hebrew underwent before every cultic action in which he took part. From this we may further get an impression of the way in which throughout his life he was not only bound by the requirements of conventional customs, but also restrained by strict standards which covered everything, from eating food to married life, from things voluntarily undertaken to those which might happen to a man unexpectedly and involuntarily, as for example the accidental touching of a dead body or of a carcase when working in the fields (Lev. 22.4, 8). This is not an arbitrary or indifferent matter, a matter of individual freedom or of self-imposed regulations. Every phenomenon and every occurrence is controlled by the sacred ruling of revered tradition and of cultic regulation.

The same is true of marriage. It goes without saying that the Hebrew will marry, for that is the natural course of events. The man cleaves to his wife (Gen. 2.24), and the woman longs for the man (Gen. 3.16). It corresponds to the divine ordering of creation: 'Be fruitful and multiply and fill the earth' (Gen. 1.28). 'Give me children, or else I die,' cries Rachel (Gen. 30.1), and even in the New Testament it is stated that the woman shall be saved through her child-bearing, if she continues in faith and love and sanctification with sobriety (I Tim. 2.15). Man and wife and children form the smallest but also most natural community. The Arabs still call the bachelor *'azab*, 'forsaken, lonely'. The Old Testament has no word for this at all, so unusual is the idea. Nor is there known the woman who remains single, or more correctly the woman who is left single, since the step to marriage always comes here from the man. Were there then no unmarried people? We do not know. It is only concerning Jeremiah that the word of God is preserved: 'Thou shalt not take thee a wife, neither shalt thou have sons or daughters in this place' (16.2) 'I sat alone because of thy hand' (15.17) is the complaint of this, the most isolated of men (1.5).

Wherever in a community everyone marries and is married, many tensions are absent. There is no mention in the Old Testament either of the tragedy of unhappy lovers who may not come together or of the tragedy of unhappily married people who do not suit one another. Only once is it related how the secondary wife of a Levite in the hill-country of Ephraim ran away and stayed four months with her father in Bethlehem. Her husband was then successful in persuading her to return (Judg. 19.1-10). It was normal to marry among one's kin. The Bedouin to-day still regard the cousin, daughter of the father's or mother's brother or sister, as the proper person for a wife. Thus it is God's dispensation that Eliezer, searching for a bride for his master's son, finds Rebecca 'my master's brother's daughter' (Gen. 24.48). Jacob too marries the daughters of his mother's brother, Leah and Rachel. In the earlier period it was permissible also to marry a half-sister, who had one parent in common, but not the other. Sarah, the wife of Abraham, was 'the daughter of my father, but not the daughter of my mother' (Gen. 20.12). To escape dishonour, Tamar, David's daughter by Maacah, was willing to marry Amnon, David's son by Ahinoam: '. . . speak unto the king; for he will not withhold me from thee' (II Sam. 13.13). At a later date, marriage with half-brothers and half-sisters was, however, strictly forbidden (Lev. 18.9).

Where the choice of a partner in marriage is governed by strict traditions,[1] the future married pair grow up aware that they are intended for one another. Marriages are more the affair of the family and of convention, than matters of strong personal inclination

[1] The choice of marriage partner and everything which goes with it as it is carried out in a modern Palestinian village is described excellently and with full detail by Hilma Granqvist, *Marriage Conditions in a Palestinian Village* (Helsinki, 1931). Cf. also the same author's *Birth and Childhood among the Arabs* (Helsinki, 1947), and *Child Problems among the Arabs* (Helsinki, 1950).

and individual choice. On the whole, therefore, the search for a wife took place without any great struggles, though accounts of exceptional individual love are not lacking. Jacob wanted Rachel, and not Leah, who, according to custom, should come to him first (Gen. 29). Shechem, the son of Hamor the Hivite, saw Dinah and violated her, and yet continued to love her (Gen. 34.1-4); whereas Amnon, sick with love for Tamar, hated the girl as soon as he had ravished her (II Sam. 13.1-15). 'Amnon hated her with exceeding great hatred; for the hatred wherewith he hated her was greater than the love wherewith he had loved her.' There can hardly be found a deeper expression of psychological insight into the nature and instability of merely sensual desire. But the most beautiful account of the devotion of true love is told of Paltiel, the son of Laish. Saul had given to David his daughter Michal as wife (I Sam. 18.20 f.), but when madness had come upon Saul and David had become a fugitive, he had taken her away from him and given her to Paltiel (I Sam. 25.44). When David became king, he demanded that Ishbaal, Saul's son, should restore Michal to him. 'Ishbaal sent and took her from her husband, even from Paltiel the son of Laish. And her husband went with her, weeping as he went, and followed her to Bahurim. Then said Abner unto him, Go, return; and he returned' (II Sam. 3.15 f.). Here we have a man whose wife loves another man (I. Sam. 18.20). She is taken away from him, and he follows her weeping as she is led away, until he is driven off by brute force.

The Hebrew was permitted to have more than one wife at a time. This may be explained on the grounds that it was originally better, in the close contacts of life, for every marriageable woman to be in proper relationship to some man, rather than that improper relationships should arise in which the children would suffer because no one would be responsible for them. We do not know how far such polygamous marriages were the fashion. The fact that a very large number of wives is recorded for some of the kings must not lead us to draw wrong conclusions. Thus David, during his rule at Hebron, had six wives,[1] whost first-born sons are noted (II Sam. 3.2-5); Solomon had many foreign wives who led him astray to their gods (I Kings 11.1-8); Abijah had fourteen wives, and twenty-two sons and sixteen daughters by them (II Chron. 13.21). At courts different customs and laws prevail from those of the ordinary people. Economic factors would in any case prevent the Hebrew from having many women in marriage at any one time, and the question of domestic peace was also involved. If a man had several wives, one could be called ṣārāh, 'enemy, rival' from the viewpoint of the others; the kind of relationship which might exist is illustrated by the experience of Elkanah. He had two wives, Hannah who was childless, and Peninnah who had children: Peninnah continually provoked Hannah because she was childless. We may imagine what Elkanah's life was like between these two women (I Sam. 1.1-7). The law forbade a man to have two sisters as wives at the same time (Lev. 18.18), for between sisters the relationship of being rival wives might well be particularly

---

[1] The political character of marriage alliances must not be overlooked. By this means David gained a firm foothold for himself, and support in families and settlements.

unhappy, though Jacob did have two sisters, Leah and Rachel, as wives at the same time.

In addition to wives with full rights, the Hebrew could also take slaves into marital relationships. Thus Sarah gave Abraham her maid Hagar, the Egyptian, because she herself was childless (Gen. 16), and Hagar, as soon as she was expecting a child by Abraham, looked down upon Sarah. Jacob, too, in addition to having sons by his two wives, had sons by their two maids Bilhah and Zilpah (Gen. 35.25-26). The Hebrew had also the right to take a woman captured in war into marital relationships (Deut. 21.10-14), but she acquired special privileges, for afterwards he was not permitted to sell her as a slave.

All these relationships bring with them complications and legal questions which are discussed in detail and need to be interpreted in the sociology of marriage and the family. Here we are only concerned to mention those matters which influenced the life-history of the Hebrew. The marriageability of the woman was limited by the time at which she ceased to be able to bear children, about her fortieth to forty-fifth year. The man could, however, enter upon new marriages and beget children to a much greater age. Abraham, who, according to the tradition, lived to one hundred and seventy-five years (Gen. 25.7), took a wife named Keturah after Sarah's death, and she became the ancestress of a whole series of Arab tribes (Gen. 25.1 ff.). Moses married a Cushite woman after the Midianite Zipporah (Num. 12.1). It is not the legendary dates which are of importance, but the fact that a Hebrew of fifty or sixty years of age married again, and that his new wife was probably twenty or twenty-five or thirty years old. At the time of this second marriage, the son of the first marriage might have been already thirty-one to forty-one years old (cf. pp. 61 ff.). The son was thus older than or about the same age as his father's new wife, and if the father died shortly after, it might well have occurred to the son to marry his father's widow. It was thus that earlier maturity (cf. pp. 61 ff.) brought the generations closer together, indeed caused them to pass one another and made prohibitions of marriage relevant and necessary which are scarcely ever needed among us (Lev. 18). By way of a concluding and summarizing comment, as we consider all the provisions and happenings in this department of life, we may say that strict custom, religious attitudes concerning the taboos on everything sexual, and the fact that marriage is regarded rather as an occasion of the family than as a matter of the inclinations and feelings of the individual, all made marriage into a convenient arrangement which knew nothing of many of our modern dangers, abnormalities and problems.

We should like to know how prevalent polygamy was and how monogamy was regarded beside it. Legally it is still possible for an orthodox Jew to enter upon more than one marriage, and it does even happen where the secular laws of the state do not prevent it. But we have no statistics available. We do, however, find in Malachi, about 400 B.C., the warning: 'Therefore take heed to your spirit, and let none break faith with the wife of his youth' (2.15). It is not so much the warning as the expression 'wife of his youth' which impresses us here. For in it we may discern how the first experience of married life, with its wonder, its joys, its dangers and its blessings, binds the young married couple together in a very special way, and that this is the real foundation of monogamy and gave it the victory over polygamy in the course of its long evolution.

The third significant community into which the young Hebrew entered was the community of law.[1] When men carry on their life in the street, before the gate, in field and pasture, in the closest contact and in daily observation of each other's affairs, we get not merely a daily interaction and friction, but judgments continually being passed on behaviour, on friendly and unfriendly attitudes, on matters which conform to tradition, to custom and law, and on those which do not. The Hebrew boy heard his father and mother, and the other adult members of the household, continually making observations and passing judgment. He himself liked to observe and to judge, and he grew up exercising this capacity. His powers of observation, his eloquence, his wit, his ability to judge were here exercised. He was proud of himself when he judged rightly, and depressed when he could not yet do so. Thus from an early age he was trained to ask about law—about what the community regards as right. Hebrew law is the law of custom almost throughout its development. As was formerly done, so men should do now. What was once decided in a complex situation was known to the old men, and they related it so that it might provide the standard for the present decision. It was heard, weighed, and its bearing, its validity and applicability discussed. What a training of the mind this provided! What a joy to be able to share in this!

[1] Cf. the appendix: 'Justice in the Gate', pp. 149 ff.

And all did indeed share in it, at least all the men, all who lived in the place, and were at home in the bond of the clan; all those at any rate who were free, and had not made themselves incapable of legal activity by guilt or offence. Law was the possession, the activity, the responsibility of the whole assembly of men, who gathered at the gate and decided what was right for each case, whenever they were summoned to it. At first the young men would listen in silence, but not without following the argument sympathetically, weighing it and the parties concerned and the points of view in their own minds. Then came the exciting moment when a young man for the first time opened his mouth as a witness,[1] or as an active participant. He felt that he too had something to say; he could see what others had overlooked. He was able to unravel, to explain, to decide, where others were at a loss. To him there fell the defence of a widow, an orphan, a small and oppressed person. His speech found a hearing, and his arguments convinced. He won a victory over a violent and powerful man by the decision of the community. What an experience this was for him! It brought an inner growth to maturity, to the consciousness that he was a free man among free men, a citizen among citizens, a real man, virtuous and worthy. Law and righteousness are the true marks of Hebrew nobility.

David boasts that he had to fight with lions and bears as a youth in the pasture (I Sam. 17.34-37). Benaiah climbed down into a cistern on a snowy day, and killed

---

[1] It must not be overlooked that, in the linguistic usage of the Old Testament, witness and judge are not strictly separated, as they are to-day, but that they are covered by one and the same word. The witness also takes part in the pronouncing of judgment, and the judge can give evidence.

a lion which had taken refuge there (II Sam. 23.20). Amos knows that everyone is stricken with fear when a lion roars within the village boundary and announces that he is out for prey (Amos 3.8), and Amos was not the only prophet who could speak about lions from his own experience. At any rate in the earlier period the large beasts of prey must have been not uncommon. After the fall of Samaria there was a plague of lions in the central part of the country—this, so the Deuteronomic historian tells us, was because nothing was known of the cultus, of the claims of the god of the land (*mishpaṭ 'ĕlōhē hā'āreṣ*) (II Kings 17.27). Around every settlement there lay the fields within the boundary, which needed cultivation. But outside these, on the uncultivable slopes of the hills, far from the village and near to the desert, which is no man's, and to the waste land—the area covered with thickets (*ya'ar*)—lay the pasture for the cattle. There were to be found the cattle, sheep and goats. There, alone and thrown on their own resources, lived the boys, the youths and young men, isolated or in small groups, and not all in a position to return every evening to the safety of the settlement. To some extent, it may be, their duties provided them with an idyllic life, with sleeping, gossiping, dreaming, playing, the laying of traps and bird nets, singing and playing on home-made shepherd flutes. But even if this were so, it filled up only a part of the day, quite apart from the night with its insecurity, the terror of uncanny noises, the threat of robbers and beasts of prey. Even during the day a band of nomads or soldiers might pass in the distance, and a watch must be kept that they did not, as they passed, take one of the flock with them. There were also cattle thieves who would creep up slowly and unobserved, would lie in wait for a shepherd to turn his back, so that a sheep, or a goat, or a cow could be quickly snatched away and taken unseen into the thickets. If the shepherd could not show a piece of an ear or two legs which he had snatched as he struggled with the thieving beast of prey (Amos 3.12), if he could not prove that he had carried out his duty of watchfulness to the utmost, he might well be responsible for the payment of the damage and at the end of his period of shepherding have lost rather than gained.

If we consider these aspects of the shepherd's life, we can see that the young Hebrew had no soft upbringing, but grew to be able-bodied and ready for a fight. It was thus that he learnt to bear arms—the staff, the club, the spear, the knife, the dagger, and, where one was obtainable, the sword. The importance of the sling is well known to us all from David and the story of his fight with Goliath. The Hebrew was an able-bodied man, and just as he had to struggle with wild beasts, thieves and foreign invaders, so he knew also how to use his weapons in single combat. Whenever the trumpet sounded to call a clan, a village, a tribe, or a whole country to war, or when one man—like Saul when Jabesh was besieged—sent messengers into every district, carrying bleeding flesh in their hands, with the threat that whoever did not respond would have his own beasts thus slaughtered (I Sam. 11.5 ff.), he was ready to answer the call. The further development of this, and the rise of a regular army, do not concern us here, but belong to the description of the Hebrew community. But in every period, the young Hebrew grew up into a fellowship of warriors, as into a fellowship of law. For in every period of Hebrew history, even in the apparently more peaceful later times, there was no lack of danger of attack, and no end to the need for defence with weapons in the hand (Neh. 4.16 ff. [Heb. 10 ff.]). He was not a man who did not know how to use a weapon. Only the valiant counted in the life of the people and with the women. Whoever wanted to be called a man must be able to handle a weapon.

After the Hebrew had entered the four communities which we have mentioned, his life was passed amid a host of daily experiences and happenings, whose great variety and diversity may be imagined, though not fully described. But before we turn to his old age and his death, there is one phenomenon which must concern us, which has hardly as yet been fully grasped. It is what the Hebrew called *sōd*. A visitor to one of our villages or small towns who watches carefully may get the impression that day after day, even week in, week out, nothing either interesting or striking happens to interrupt the monotony of the regular, ordinary events. In the same way, perhaps even more clearly, an observer might have had such an impression in a Hebrew village or town. At early dawn, the life of the place awoke. The hand-mill was turned under the hands of the women, the meal was ground for the daily food, and the grating sound was perhaps accompanied by a long drawn-out monotonous work-song. The girls went in a long line[1] to the well or to the

---

[1] In Palestine two or more people do not walk beside one another, but one behind the other. This is clearly expressed in the Hebrew preposition *'achărē*, and also in New Testament Greek in ὀπίσω. But the meaning is altered and spiritualized when the New Testament translators say 'follow' where they ought to say 'accompany'.

spring to fetch water, and the shepherd drove his animals out to the pasture. The men, and at harvest-time, the women and children too, went out to the fields, to plough and sow, to water and weed, to reap and gather, while women and children combed and prepared the flax and washed the wool, ready for spinning and weaving. The potter moulded the clay and shaped the pots, for baking and drying. The dyer dyed and the fuller dressed the cloth. Each did his work, not with undue haste, for the clock and the pay-packet were not there to speed the hands. At midday there was a break for sleep, and in the late afternoon the day's work came early to an end. The lack of sufficient nourishment meant also the lack of strength to undertake too arduous a task. Each man worked as much as was necessary to maintain life. No one asked more. The urge to continuous effort, which affects us all so intensely, was completely missing. The best thing in life is what the modern Arab calls *kēf*, which we entirely lack, but which was certainly known and familiar to the Hebrew—the ability to sit quietly, inactive, not even thinking, let alone worrying or planning, in attitudes whose relaxation and comfort we can hardly achieve with the greatest of effort. For about six months in the year it did not rain at all, and even in the other six months there were many hours of the day when the fiercely shining sun dried the soil so quickly that you could only lean against any stone or wall or projecting piece of ground without care, and relax in *kēf*. 'Each man under his vine and under his fig tree from Dan to Beer-sheba' (I Kings 4.25 [Heb. 5.5]).

    Night comes early. Palestine lies so far south that only

a short twilight precedes it. Then each man found his bed and slept till the day dawned. The one who could not sleep—usually the fate of the old—may 'meditate in his law day and night' (Ps. 1.2). Almost every Psalm expresses the prayer of those for whom the night, almost equal in length summer and winter,[1] lasts too long for them to sleep right through. Then, unnoticed by the household, who are well used to it, there might be heard the praises and thanksgivings, the laments and questions, sounding in dull tones from the houses on to the street. There the watchman heard them as he went regularly upon his rounds, so that the sleepless might count the hours as he went by. 'Watchman, what of the night? Watchman, will the night soon be over?' (Isa. 21.11).

But before night thus brought quietness to every street and open place, two things happened in which everybody shares. The one is the meal, the other is *sōd*. Whereas among us it is possible almost everywhere to think of three meal-times in the day—breakfast, midday meal, and evening meal—in the whole Mediterranean area, and especially in the simpler and agricultural areas, there are only two mealtimes. Breakfast is missing. The first, indeed the most important hours of work up to midday, when the heat of the day enforces a cessation from work, are passed fasting. This is indicated in fact by the English use of the word 'breakfast' for the morning meal, which was originally not taken before the beginning of the day's work. The French use the word *déjeuner*, from the Latin *de* and *jejunare*, that is, make an end of fasting. Both these modern words originally indicated the early

[1] Cf. p. 72 n.

midday meal. Among the Hebrews, this meal at about the middle of the day was hardly of any great importance. The chief meal-time, and no doubt the only one for the poor and in times of scarcity of food, was taken in the early evening, probably about two hours before sunset. That this was the chief meal is still expressed in the Italian name for it, *la cena*. It is the Greek τὸ κοινόν the 'common' meal,[1] in which every member of the household joins together after they have all finished the day's work. With it they begin to rest from their work. When it is over, there will still be an hour, perhaps two, before the falling darkness compels everyone to go to bed, for no lights worthy of mention for rooms or streets were available. What happened during this time? The children might well play till they were tired. The youths and girls, the sexes strictly separated, might perhaps sing, for the Hebrews were a people of song-lovers, and dance. But what of the older men and the aged? This was the time for *sōd*. What then was *sōd*?

Jeremiah laments that he is not permitted to sit in the *sōd* of those who rejoice: because of God's hand, he must sit separated (Jer. 15.17). The false prophets may not be in the '*sōd* of my people', says God by Ezekiel (Ezek. 13.9). The pious man will praise God with his whole heart in the *sōd* of those who do right (Ps. 111.1). What *sōd* means here, can be translated as 'circle'. It was the free meeting together in time of

[1] In French the phrase '*la Sainte Cène*' has become the normal expression for the Lord's Supper, and rightly so, since the last meal which Jesus took with his disciples was an evening meal, and the time at which it was taken is determined by the fact that after the meal there was still time to sing the praises (*Hallels*—Psalms 113-118) during daylight, and then for them to go out of the city to the Mount of Olives (Matt. 26.30).

leisure of the adult men, while the housewives and mothers, tired no doubt but unrelaxing, still exerted themselves in the last business of their daily work. It can be seen by the traveller in the Italian or Greek countryside where, in the leisure of the evening, until it grows dark, the men sit together in the open, around an old tree, by the murmuring brook, or in the open space at the entrance to the village. They need neither inn nor assembly room, neither society nor club, but sit in free fellowship together. If one is not present, the others miss him. If two have quarrelled, they stay away, and everyone is pleased when they are reconciled and take their places again. The one who recovers from a long illness, or who has travelled away on important business, or has been called up for military service, is greeted with pleasure when his familiar face reappears. For although there is no compulsion to attend, it is proper to appear in the evening circle. It is noticed when one is not there, and the question as to the reason for absence goes around the circle with astonishment, or anxiety, or perplexity.

If we ask what this circle means and does, then the answer is that it is the place where the news of the day is exchanged. It is the place where the plans for the coming days and for projects which lie ahead are discussed. It is the place for conversation. When the Bedouin crouch on the ground together in the evening around the camp-fire, the story-tellers and singers lift their voices, to recite long poems, skilful songs, stories of the heroic deeds of old time. No doubt this happened in Israel too. The Song of Deborah must have been thus handed down for centuries, and similarly the ancient sagas, stories and legends of the desert wanderings, of the patriarchs, and of the great flood. But in addition—and this seems to me to have been almost unrecognized up till now—there was a place for the handing on of the ancient wisdom of life. The man who is wise (ḥākām) is in the first place in Hebrew thought a man who understands a thing, and understands it properly. Then he is one who has experienced much and therefore knows for himself how one should act in a given situation. Experience is wisdom. All the wisdom of which the Old Testament speaks is practical wisdom. It was handed on in the evening in the circle of men. This circle will have been the place of origin of the 'proverbs', that is, those proverbial sayings of which the Book of Proverbs offers a great wealth, and which, if we look closely, have quite definite forms.

One of these forms may be singled out for special mention here. The men sat or lay around in a circle, the older and more respected in the centre, the younger around them, and on the outer edge a few youths who would not be allowed to join in the talk for another two or three years, and even then only with diffidence, and could hardly wait until this moment comes.

The day's affairs have already been discussed, and those things too which the near future promises or threatens: a good harvest, sufficient rain or a drought, the first signs of a plague of locusts, the appearance of a lion or a bear in the neighbourhood. All this has been talked over, and for a moment there is silence. Then a voice is heard:

> 'Two things have I asked of thee;
> Deny me *them* not before I die.'

At once another grasps what is meant, and replies:

> 'Remove far from me vanity and lies:
> Give me neither poverty nor riches;
> Feed me with my due portion of bread' (30.7 f.).[1]

No one quite knows why the first man said what he did, for it had no connection with what was being discussed, and the answer given by the second man has no connection either. But this does not matter. Everyone understands what is meant. A conversation has been set in motion in which everyone takes part with interest, as questioner, as responder, or simply as listener. A third says:

> 'There be three things which are too wonderful for me,'

and as he pauses, to see if anyone knows the answer, a fourth joins in:

> 'Yes, four which I know not;'

But now some know how the first question is to be answered, and one of them names the three things:

> 'The way of an eagle in the air;
> The way of a serpent upon a rock;
> The way of a ship in the midst of the sea,'

Whether anyone can name the fourth thing, and whether he thinks it proper to name it, is uncertain. Perhaps the answer is laid as a punishment upon the one who was thoughtless enough to dare the allusion (30.18 f.).

There are also much simpler forms of this cross talk,

---

[1] All the passages which follow are from the Book of Proverbs.

but in them too can be revealed good taste, judgment, experience and familiarity with what the ancients said, and also readiness in the invention of new answers to old questions, and even humour and mockery.

One says: 'Like moths in a garment and worms in wood', and another replies: 'So trouble eats up the heart of a man' (25.20 LXX).

One begins: 'The legs of the lame hang loose', and another finishes: 'So does a proverb in a fool's mouth' (26.7).

One says: 'A whip for the horse, a bridle for the ass', and another completes it with: 'And a rod for the back of the fool' (26.3).

One says: 'A dog returns to his vomit', and another answers: 'A fool, who repeats his folly twice over' (26.11).

One says : 'The door turns upon its hinges', and the answer comes: 'And the sluggard upon his bed' (26.14). A third adds: 'The sluggard buries his hand in the dish', and a fourth takes up his words and completes the saying: 'He is too lazy to bring it again to his mouth' (26.15).

Of the thousands of proverbs which were thus spoken in the *sōd*, enjoyed, thought over quietly as men returned to their homes, and often taken to heart, only a few hundred have survived. Anyone who looks through them carefully, and sets them out as we have done in question and answer, as protasis and apodosis, in order to grasp their *Sitz im Leben* (Gunkel), will discover that the examples given above provide only a faint impression of the richness of their forms and variations. There is a whole series of identical opening phrases with varying sequels, and a similar series where the opening phrase varies while the sequels are the same. There are simple and elaborate comparisons; pictures with their moral application drawn out. There are many which we should describe as riddles, or which could easily be turned into riddles, and and among them riddles with simple obvious solutions, and others with double meanings, some with harmless and some with biting meanings, some simple, some with catches.

It is not our concern here to discuss the special characteristics and what we must call the stylized form of the proverbs, for our purpose in this connection is a different one. It is our concern to show how we have here conversation, intellectual activity, and education, not on the same level as the academy of a Socrates and a Plato, nor as the books of Egyptian teaching,[1] but having a great significance for the intellectual life of the Hebrew, and particularly for that of the mature and ageing Hebrew. If we compare more modern forms of conversation with it, we cannot help envying its vitality.

At length there comes old age and death. When does old age come? With the women the capacity to bear children passes (Gen. 18.13). For the man, the decisive point is that his hair turns grey. His strength diminishes, his head becomes white, and he does not notice it (Hos. 7.9). It comes upon him unawares that he cannot do this or that without panting. A load is too heavy for him, a journey too far, a goal too distant, for his

---

[1] On this cf. now Hellmut Brunner, 'Die Weisheitsliteratur', in *Handbuch der Orientalistik*, Vol. I *Ägyptologie*, part II: *Literatur* (1952), pp. 90-110.

eyes also begin to become uncertain, as Isaac was to discover (Gen. 27.1). The greater the age, the further the capacity for taking part in the pleasures of life decreases. 'I am this day fourscore years old' says Barzillai to David; 'Can I discern between what is pleasant and what is unpleasant? Can I still taste what I eat or what I drink? Can I any more listen with enjoyment to the voices of singing men and singing women? Wherefore then should I be yet a burden unto my lord the king? I will go home and die in my own city, at the grave of my father and my mother' (II Sam. 19.35-37 [Heb. 36-38]).

It is the wealthy man of property who speaks. There come before his mind the pleasures which have gone from him in old age, and which he used to enjoy. The average Hebrew, that is the poor small farmer, would think less of this aspect of old age. As one may still hear it said by such people, especially on the land, he would feel that he has become useless. This has a double meaning. On the one hand it indicates that he thinks of himself as useless, of no value, because he cannot any longer do much at work. On the other hand, however, it means that he is useless to his own people; he can be dispensed with; he has become a superfluous member of the group because he is only a consumer and no longer a producer.

It is in this context that we must set the command: 'Honour thy father and thy mother that thy days may be long upon the land which Yahweh thy God giveth thee' (Ex. 20.12, Deut. 5.16). Here belongs also the instruction: 'Thou shalt rise up before the hoary head, and honour the face of the old man, and thou shalt fear thy God' (Lev. 19.32). Similarly the word of promise

(Isa. 46.4) can be given its full meaning: 'Even to old age I am he, and even to hoar hairs will I carry you' (says God). Here belongs too the legal requirement which was renewed in the seventh century, according to which the parents of a son who persistently opposes their discipline, and does not improve his behaviour when he is warned by father and mother, may bring him before the judgment seat at the gate and lay a complaint before the community there. If this complaint is found to be justified, the son is stoned (Deut. 21.18-21). Even as late as the nineteenth century this law, admittedly in the somewhat milder form of a sentence to several years' service in the galleys, was still effective in the penal system of Italy.

If all this is taken into account, the picture we get of old age, as the Hebrew experienced it, is not so bright as we might be tempted to think. Perhaps it also indicates the exact nuance of the expression that 'so-and-so was old and died full of years', as it is said of Abraham (Gen. 25.8), Isaac (Gen. 35.29), David, of whose last days we are given more detail (I Kings 1 and 2, I Chron. 23.1), and Job (42.17). To die is the way of all the earth, says David (I Kings 2.2). One day everything must come to an end. All is over. Death comes. In a community where there was so much death, and where death took place like birth in the open, with everyone sharing in the events, little was known of those terrors of death to which Paul's words refer.

Burial was the affair of the relatives: 'his kinsman, the one who buries him' (Amos 6.10). The grave was soon ready, and the burial immediately and rapidly completed. The community had only been together for about three hours when the men who had carried out the body of Ananias to bury it, came back (Acts 5.1-10). Decomposition sets in so rapidly that such a quick completion of the necessary rites is essential. The mourning rites and the period of mourning last therefore all the longer. Joseph and the Egyptians 'wept for' the death of Jacob for seven days (Gen. 50.10), after the Egyptians had already wept for him for seventy days. This may be the Egyptian rule, and it may be that the importance of Joseph resulted in the observance of a longer period of mourning for his father than was otherwise normal. But what is more, mourning as we describe it to-day is not at all the same thing as mourning as the Hebrew knew it. For us, mourning is the expression of an inner feeling, a particular mood of the mind, which suffers from separation from the dead and from the change in our own situation brought about by death, to which the mourner has to adjust his inner life. For the Hebrew, mourning was a much more tangible thing. When Joseph and his brothers held a mourning for his father for seven days, this does not mean that they wept for seven days because their minds could not become reconciled to their father's death. Jacob looked with complete calm towards the day when he would be gathered to his ancestors (Gen. 49.29). The lament for the dead[1] means rather that those who survived met together and wept for seven days, in the morning and perhaps in the evening, as devout Jews still do to-day. Why do they weep? We must observe first that weeping among us is a quite involuntary outburst of feeling,

---

[1] The whole subject of mourning rites is discussed by Hedwig Jahnow, *Das hebräische Leichenlied im Rahmen der Völkerdichtung* (1923).

which we are rather inclined to suppress, whereas among the Hebrews, and not only among them, weeping was very much dependent upon the will. We too know of people who can pour out tears whenever they wish, and only thus can we understand the demand: 'Cover the altar with weeping' (Mal. 2.13). The Hebrew could weep whenever he wished. He wept easily and frequently, and his weeping was a deliberate ritual, not an involuntary expression of feeling. So when death came, men did not weep because of their feelings—though this may also have happened—but because it was customary and seemly.

Why then was it customary? The dead were unclean and men were afraid of them. This went so far that in the priestly law (Lev. 21) it is laid down that a priest may only 'profane' himself for his nearest blood relatives, mother, father, son, daughter, brother and sister, provided she is still a virgin. To 'profane' himself means here to take part in mourning rites. Why is this so? If the dead are called 'unclean' it is the same as saying that they are uncanny. They are uncanny because they belong to other powers, the powers of death. These were not originally under the power of God, and an echo of this attitude remained for a long time. But how was this uncanny nature of the dead experienced?

The dead could show themselves to the living. They appeared, they might also be made to appear, as the story of the witch of Endor shows (I Sam..28). A picture of the Hebrew community, which we are not giving here, would not be complete if it did not include the conjurors of the dead, both male and female. But what does this appearance of the dead mean? It is a very generally known psychological fact that a man who has been particularly strongly bound to another in mind and spirit, and who therefore suffers a violent shock to his whole way of life by the death of the other, may believe that he hears, sees, or even touches the dead man in dreams, awake, in the twilight, on sudden awakening, at times when they were long accustomed to be together. It is the critical mind which recognizes that these experiences are the result of a powerful reminiscence; the uncritical takes them as actual and real. The appearance of the dead then produces a terrifying, uncanny effect. They have been seen to die, they have been seen to be buried; they are not there in bright daylight where they were normally met. For they are in fact dead. Then all at once they are present; they become visible, they nod, they call, they question, they warn and then they are no longer there. How should that not be uncanny?

For dying, the Hebrews used the lovely expression: 'To be gathered to one's ancestors, one's fathers'. For it was normal to bury the dead among his own, where his predecessors were buried. It is for this reason that punishment of crimes by death was normally by burning or stoning. If a man was stoned, he was covered with stones (*rāgam*) so that nothing of him was left there. If a man was burnt, there remained only a little pile of ashes, nothing at all, for he no longer existed. Thus it was ensured that he could not reappear. For even the dearest person, when once he is dead, is a member of another world, the realm of death, and therefore uncanny, and something to be avoided, 'unclean'. It is thus that the real meaning of the observances and customs of mourning may be explained. They were settlements with the dead, methods of release from them.

The dead person is now in Sheol. It is sometimes stated that this means the underworld, the Hades of the Greeks. But this is only approximately true. Sheol, as has only recently been proved,[1] is really the 'not-land', the 'land which is not a land', the realm which is not. Thither the dead go. There 'there is no remembrance of thee: in the not-land who shall give thee thanks?' (Ps. 6.5 [Heb. 6]). This not-land was by no means the hell of later times. The form, nature, and meaning of hell were the product only of later ages.

The dead man remained in the not-land only for a certain time, and it is in fact possible to say how long. It was for just as long as there were still men to whom he appeared, who still knew his name. When that time was over, then it was as if he had never been. The life of the Hebrew was at an end. Only God knows of him always.

[1] Cf. my Lexicon under the relevant root.

6

HOW THE HEBREW THOUGHT I

It is difficult enough to give even a moderately graphic and coherent picture of the way in which the Hebrew lived, and of the course of his life, as he shared it with the general run of his fellows, but the difficulties are much greater when we attempt to describe how the Hebrew thought, in a way which is in some measure both comprehensible and generally valid. For in the realm of mental life the characteristics of the individual vary much more sharply than in the physical. The mental outlook of men is always much less easy to comprehend. The difference, too, between the mental outlook of a group of men of the past—and in this case such a remote past—and the complex make-up of the modern man is enormous, and is also, just because it is a matter of inner experience, extremely difficult to tie down to words and concepts. It would certainly not be feasible to attempt to treat in one narrowly defined system the different aspects of the Hebrew's way of thought. On many points there would be no real information, and the picture of the whole would appear lifeless, a mere sequence of notes contributing little or nothing. Much more enriching, because more alive, would be the method of setting out first a few striking features and attempting to understand them, so that we may then go on to speak of more profound experiences and mental patterns.

In the collection of laws which is called Deuteronomy, dating from the end of the seventh century, we find certain regulations concerning the formation of the militia (20.1-9). Anyone who has built a new house but has not yet occupied it, is to stay at home. Anyone who has planted a vineyard, but has never yet harvested from it, may not go with the army. Anyone who has married a wife, but has not yet taken her home, is not to take part in the campaign. These regulations show that humaneness which belongs to the basic outlook of the whole collection of laws, but it has long been recognized that their origin is not a matter of humanity, but of religious belief. The builder, the vine-grower, the newly-married man stood under the sway of divine powers which exercised control over building, over the new planting, or over the recent marriage, and which would not let it go unpunished if the man who had stepped into their domain did not remain in it for his proper time. He would fall in battle and thus weaken the militia instead of strengthening it.[1] Now there is added to these regulations yet another: 'What man is there that is fearful and fainthearted? Let him go and return unto his house, lest his brethren's heart melt as his heart' (20.8). Some people have regarded this regulation as unrealistic, and have been amused by it. But it may be shown to be serious and by no means unpractical.

One of the assurances given by God to his people runs: 'I will send the hornet before thee which shall

---

[1] Cf. F. Schwally, *Semitische Kriegsaltertümer*, Part I: 'Der Heilige Krieg im alten Israel' (1901).

drive out the Canaanite from before thee. I will not drive them out from before thee in one year, lest the land become desolate, and the beast of the field multiply against thee' (Ex. 23.28 f.). It has only recently been recognized[1] that, here and in other passages which belong in this connection, it cannot be 'hornet' which is meant, but that the word which has been thus translated means rather 'depression, lack of courage'. God sends discouragement before his people. It comes upon the enemies of Israel, and the enemies yield. An ancient Greek would speak here of 'panic terror'. Discouragement may fall upon a whole army. One man feels it first, and passes it to his neighbour without speaking a word. Like an infection it runs through the ranks, until this fear takes possession of everyone and makes them incapable of fighting or resisting. It is this condition which God will bring upon the enemies of Israel. In order to avoid this condition, this infection, those who are fainthearted are removed from the militia of Israel before the beginning of the battle. No moral judgment is passed upon them. They are just sought out objectively and the danger of infection from them is thus avoided. They are not cowardly in the modern sense of the word, which is derogatory, and indeed implies reproach. They are, however, cowards in the ancient sense, that is, 'destined by fate to death or to misfortune'. The important thing for us to notice in this connection is that the Hebrew is liable to such psychic infection. What is felt by the individual, his disposition of mind and its effects, is transmitted to his environment, and the environment carries the individual with it. The Hebrew lives with

[1] L. Köhler, *Kleine Lichter* (1945), pp. 17 ff.

his own mental disposition within that of his environment. He transmits his disposition to the group; and the group in return carries him into its mood.

There are several examples of this. Saul met a group of *nabis*—we use this word to distinguish the associations of prophets from individual prophets—who were carrying out practices to induce ecstasy with 'psaltery, and a timbrel, and a pipe, and a harp' (I Sam. 10.5). Immediately the ecstasy was transmitted to him. On another occasion he sent out messengers to fetch back David. The messengers came to Samuel, who was leading an ecstatic band of *nabis*. Immediately the ecstasy fell upon the messengers. Saul sent a second group of messengers, and they too were seized by the ecstasy. The same thing happened to a third group. Eventually Saul went himself, and he too fell into ecstasy and—here we discover just what is meant—Saul 'lay down naked all that day and all that night' (I Sam. 19.20-24).

Such occurrences are not related just once or twice. Four hundred *nabis* were gathered around the king of Israel. The question was whether he should undertake a campaign against Ramoth-Gilead. The four hundred cried out in chorus, and no doubt with constant repetition: 'Go up; Yahweh shall deliver it into the hand of the king' (I Kings 22.6). The false *nabis* who were Jeremiah's opponents would have cried out similarly. The seventy elders associated with Moses also fell into ecstasy (Num. 11.25). But this did not merely happen to the *nabis*, and it was not only a matter of religious ecstasy. An opponent of David gave out the political battle-cry of falling away from David. At his word 'all the men of Israel fell away from following David' (II Sam. 20.1 f.). The town of Jabesh was hard pressed by the Ammonites. They sent messengers over Jordan to their confederates with a request for help. Saul hewed in pieces the oxen with which he was just returning from the fields, and sent messengers throughout the whole land with the steaming flesh. 'Whosoever cometh not forth . . . so shall it be done unto his oxen. And terror from Yahweh fell on the people, and they came out as one man' (I Sam. 11.7). These examples will suffice. They confirm the statement that the Hebrew is liable to infection by mass excitement.

But this assertion must immediately be followed by its opposite, if the picture is not to be distorted. The Hebrew was capable of standing quite alone, departing from normal behaviour, from tradition, from his diffidence at the unusual, abandoning common sense and every other normal practice, and going his own individual way. We give a few examples of this, whose full significance has rarely been recognized.

There was Micaiah, the son of Imlah (I Kings 22.7-28) who was known to his king because he did not prophesy good to him—that is, something which he wanted to hear—but evil, that is, what God's truth commanded. Micaiah, son of Imlah, at first mockingly imitated the four hundred *nabis*, calling out just as they did. But when the king himself ordered him to speak 'nothing but the truth' his word sounded quite differently. He was struck on the cheek by one of the courtiers for it, and was put in prison by the king. But he remained unmoved. Here stands the individual against the many. Here the Hebrew shows himself capable of resisting being carried away by the many. The same receptiveness of mind, which in the crowd sweeps away individual thought, here shows itself open to the voice of God, to the call to go his own way and to remain true to the right, even if that means blows and imprisonment. It is the same with Nathan when he retorts to the king's adultery: 'Thou art the man' (II Sam. 12.7). It is the same with Amos against the priest Amaziah (7.10-17). It is the same with Isaiah when men mock his words with their ṣaw lĕṣaw qaw lĕqaw (28.10-12); and so also with many of the prophets in many such conflicts with the crowd.

It could be objected that these are prophets, exceptional men, with an exceptional commission resulting from an exceptional call (Jer. 1.4-10). We may therefore take two examples of laymen. David took away the wife of Uriah the soldier in a cruel act of adultery, and she bore him a child. But the child had to die. Strangely enough, a new, unexpected feature appears in the character of David. He clings to this child. When it lies sick to death, he fasts in order to pray for its life. Even at night, he does not take off the hair shirt which was the mark of his prayer and repentance, and does not go to his bed but lies upon the bare earth. But the child has to die. On the seventh day of its illness it does die. The courtiers are afraid to bring to the king the news of its death, for if during the child's illness he would not listen to those around him because of his anxiety for the child, what would he do now that the inevitable fate had come? David perceives from the whispering of the courtiers that the child is dead. What does he do? He gets up, washes himself, anoints himself, puts on other clothes, prays in the temple, and allows them to set food before him. David acts contrary to all expectations, contrary to all the customs of mourning for the dead, and to his astounded entourage he gives the quite rational and sensible explanation: 'I shall go to him, but he shall not return to me' (II Sam. 12.15-23). Here an individual detaches himself completely from the custom and way of thought of his surroundings and his own time, and acts in an individual fashion.

The story of David belongs to the earliest period of the Hebrew man, the book of Daniel to the latest, the final stage. There we have the story of the three men in the furnace. It is a legend, but the attitude of mind and the sentiments of the phrase with which we are now concerned are not affected by that. For the time of the book of Daniel, this attitude is historical. Nebuchadrezzar has set up a golden image and has commanded that at the sound of music everyone shall fall down and worship the image. Whoever does not, will be thrown into the burning furnace. Daniel's three companions, three devout Jews, do not fall down. The king commands them to carry out his order. They refuse. If they are thrown into the furnace 'our God whom we serve is able to deliver us'. And there follows the final refusal: 'But if not, let it be known unto thee, O king, that we will not worship the golden image' (Dan. 3.1-18). 'We will not.' Even if God does not save them, even if they must be destroyed, even if they lose everything, they will nevertheless not do what they are not allowed to do and do not wish to do. There is in the whole of the Bible no prouder statement, no more faithful committal to the truth, no more steadfast endurance in that which a man has acknowledged to be right and true, no more persistent determination to do only what the inner conscience commands. The same Hebrew who can be carried away by the movement of the crowd, so that he becomes only a small impersonal part of that crowd, can detach himself completely from every influence of environment, tradition, custom, and external threat, and remain true to himself alone. On the one side there is an involuntary carrying away, on the other the plainest independence, ready for any sacrifice or loss. Between these two poles, the mental life of the Hebrew moves.

But what have these two opposite poles in common? Or are we here dealing with a dichotomy in the mind which leads a man first one way and then the other? This inadequate explanation will only do if every other is unsatisfactory, or if no other can be found. But it seems to me that there is a satisfactory explanation. We find it in a particularly developed receptiveness of the Hebrew spirit, which is on the whole strange to us in the West. It is deeply affected by every external impression. It is quicker, but not only quicker but also more strongly and more passionately moved and sensitive in the highest degree. That is why Saul is carried away by ecstasy. That is why David at the death of his child acts differently, in his own particular manner. That is why the three say 'we will not'. It is all so much more passionate than is normal to us.

This same passionate spirit also shows itself elsewhere. Jonah the son of Amittai receives the commission to speak against the city of Nineveh. The first thing which he does is to run away from God. Instead of going east, he enters a ship to flee to the west. This fails, and he is brought back to where he started. He receives the commission a second time, and this time carries it out. He meets with overwhelming success.

The whole of Nineveh, men and beasts, offers repentance. So God forgives the sinful city which he was intending to destroy. And Jonah? There comes over him now a remarkable change of heart. He reproaches God: 'Did I not know it', and then 'Take my life from me, for it is better for me to die than to live' (4.2 f.).

It could be said that this is a prophetic legend, and that this change of heart fits in with the legend. But the remarkable fact is that the same process is described elsewhere too. It must be characteristic of the mind of the Hebrew. Elijah on Carmel had a mighty contest with the *nabis* of the god Baal, which ended in triumph for him. In exaltation Elijah ran before the horses of the king the whole way from Carmel to Jezreel. When Jezebel then threatens him 'If you are Elijah, I am Jezebel', all his sense of power evaporates; 'he requested for himself that he might die; and said, It is enough; now, Lord, take away my life' (I Kings 18.1-19.4). Again we have that rapid and far-reaching change from exaltation to depression.

The same tension in the expression of moods reveals itself also in other features. When Delilah nagged Samson day after day with her inquisitive questioning, he was 'vexed unto death' (Judg. 16.16). The longing of Amnon for his half-sister Tamar made him feel really ill (II Sam. 13.2). 'Hope deferred maketh the heart sick' (Prov. 13.12). 'A broken spirit drieth up the bones' (Prov. 17.22). God himself is not free of this intensity and changeability of feeling. The prophet makes God say that he is weary of bearing unasked-for worship (Isa. 1.14). But this is not the strongest expression of such feeling. Anyone who carefully examines the complaints of Jeremiah and the charges of Job will find in them much stronger outbursts of mental passion.

Thus it may be consistently observed that the mental life of the Hebrew is marked by great excitability and strong feeling. He faces life alert, passionate, almost without restraint. The further question is: how does he deal with life? To find the answer we must not limit ourselves to the consideration of mental processes, but take note of how he understands life as a whole, and how he organizes his own life as a result.

7

HOW THE HEBREW THOUGHT II

THE Bible begins with two so-called 'creation narratives', of which the second (Gen. 2.4 ff.) is older and was recorded about 1000 B.C. or after, whereas the later (Gen. 1.1 ff.) came into existence in about 550, though it contains clear indications that some of its features belong to a much earlier period. In one point, the two stories differ essentially. The second, older narrative relates that God made a single man to be the watchman and gardener of the divine garden, and that he then decided to give the man a companion in the woman 'who should be meet for him'. The first, but later narrative relates that God created the plants and animals, and in order that they might preserve their kind beyond the life-cycle of the individual, he gave them the gift of fruitfulness, that is to say, reproductiveness. He thus created—this is the obvious meaning—several of each kind of plant and each species of animal, an indefinite number of each, so that the kinds should be preserved continually by their innate fruitfulness. God also proceeded in the same manner when he created man. Under the influence of the second, older, creation narrative, the first and later one has been understood to mean that God created only one single man and his wife with him. But this is not stated, nor does it fit into the context of the narrative. In fact the contrary is stated: 'Let us make man[1] . . . male and female created he them' (not: a man and a woman) (Gen. 1.26-27).

To these first men God gives two commissions. These are the first commandments in the Bible, and they apply to all men of every age and clime. The first commission runs: 'Be fruitful and multiply' (Gen. 1.28). Just like the plants and animals, men, once created by God, are to hand on their life by their own fertility. The second commission runs: 'Fill the earth and subdue it' (Gen. 1.28). This is the commission to establish civilization. It applies to all men, and it embraces every age. There is no human activity which is not covered by it. The man who found himself with his family on an unprotected plain exposed to ice-cold wind and first laid a few stones one upon the other, and invented the wall, the basis of all architecture, was fulfilling this command. The woman who first pierced a hole in a hard thorn or a fishbone and threaded a piece of animal sinew through it in order to be able to join together a few shreds of skin, and so invented the needle, sewing, the beginning of all the art of clothing, was also fulfilling this command. Down to the present day, all the instructing of children, every kind of school, every script, every book, all our technology, research, science and teaching, with their methods and instruments and institutions, are nothing other than the fulfilment of this command. The whole

---

[1] *'Adam* here is a collective term, and *'ōthō* which depends upon it must also be understood as collective: this is a point which should never have been misunderstood.

of history, all human endeavour, comes under this sign, this biblical phrase.

That is its objective aspect. But there is also a subjective side to it. It belongs inescapably to the nature of every man that he should come to terms with life. He must seek to come to terms inwardly with everything which he encounters, whether it be a speck of dust in his eye, or a flood which threatens the life of himself and his family. It is not that he should really come to terms with it completely that matters, for none of us does. But that he endeavours to come to terms with it is of the very essence of existence. We all search after the meaning of life, and not only its meaning as a whole but also the meaning of each of its individual manifestations. The nature of a man is recognizable from the way in which he comes to terms inwardly with things. The spirit of a community is recognizable in the way in which the community as a whole comes to terms with things. So now, in order to comprehend in some measure the real spirit of the Hebrew, we may ask how he stands in relation to the great manifestations of life, and in this we go from the external to the internal, from the general to the personal experience.

An eagle stirs up its nest, it hovers over its young (Deut. 32.11). It teaches them to fly. It hovers not from fear, but because only so can it hold itself over the helpless young, who are making no headway. When they grow tired, it sweeps under them as they fall, catches them and carries them into the nest. Exactly so, the spirit of God 'hovered anxiously' over the surface of the waters, when God created heaven and earth (Gen. 1.2). Why did the spirit of God hover anxiously? We must go back to the Babylonian myth which is here echoed in order to understand. In the myth, the world was wrested from the primeval waters,[1] it is assailed by the forces of chaos which threaten to engulf it. This story, which modern readers have passed over rapidly as meaningless, is in fact of great significance. Neither the coming into existence of our world, nor its continued existence, is automatic, but the earth, the firm land, has its existence continually threatened by the onslaught of the sea. Evidence for this runs right through the Old Testament. 'I have placed the sand for the bound of the sea, by a perpetual decree, that it cannot pass it' (Jer. 5.22). 'Who stillest the roaring of the seas, the roaring of their waves' (Ps. 65.7 [Heb. 8]). These quotations are neither outworn mythology, nor mere poetic figures of speech. They are facts in the consciousness of the Hebrew. The world of men is continually threatened[2] and assailed by the destructive powers of chaos. If God were not there, chaos might become master of the earth, and disaster would be upon us. Thus, deep in his consciousness there slumbers a continual insecurity, and one which sometimes becomes wakeful and alive. Whether it is a suspicion, or clear consciousness, whether it is an echo of the past or a foreboding of future fear, which will one day be real, this vague awareness of cosmic insecurity forms the basis of the Hebrew's feeling about the world.

[1] The fact that God creates light—independent of the daylight which the sun gives—provides security. Chaos can now do nothing more, and God can now divide the world-waters so that the earth, 'the dry land' may appear (Gen. 1.3 f., 6 f., 9).

[2] The words of the Psalms 'Then the waters had overwhelmed us . . . the proud waters' (Ps. 124.4 f.) and 'The waters compassed me about, even to the soul, the deep was round about me' (Jonah 2.5 [Heb. 2.6]) presuppose the idea of the waters of the primeval deep, of chaos, not the ordinary waters.

Two further important points follow. For modern man, experiencing as he does the movement of the year by the calendar, day and night by the clock, and lunar and solar eclipses by means of astronomer's predictions (if we can still say that we experience these events), evening and morning, summer and winter, sunshine and eclipse, rainfall and drought, alternate with the commonplace regularity of clockwork. None of us asks whether it really must happen as it does. But the Hebrew still lives quite near in mind and feeling to those beginnings of mankind when, with real tension, men asked whether what happened yesterday or last year really would happen to-day or this year. Will the sun rise? Will the rains come? Will harvest follow on seed-time? In a whole host of myths and stories we can still detect that tremendous tension, so important for life, which is expressed in these and similar questions. The word of God after the flood: 'While the earth remaineth, seed-time and harvest, and cold and heat, summer and winter, and day and night shall not cease' (Gen. 8.22) is thus not arbitrary, but effective. It is not automatic, but a marvellous word from God. It is not just a beautiful saying, but a serious promise. Nor is it quite certain that this promise of God's was strong enough always to remove from the ancient Hebrew's mind the gnawing uncertainty and anxiety about the world.

For at least the eclipses of sun and moon were always taken as signs of the coming downfall of the world. 'The stars of heaven do not give their light; the sun is darkened in his going forth, and the moon does not cause her light to shine' (Isa. 13.10). This is the sign that the day of the Lord is coming 'to make the land a desolation, and to destroy the sinners thereof out of it'. Even to-day the effects of this outlook may be observed in popular beliefs.[1] Thus every eclipse of the moon, and even more every eclipse of the sun, brought terror to the mind. If rain does not come, dismay comes upon men's hearts. If there is drought—in I Kings 17.1 a drought of three years is reported from the time of Elijah[2]—and famine with the drought, then anxiety approaching despair shows in every eye. Will the rain ever come again—rain, and food, and enough to eat?

Famine is bad enough, but when once it is over it may be soon forgotten. An earthquake is much worse. Palestine is definitely an earthquake area and always has been. What this means can be seen by what happened at three o'clock in the afternoon of July 11, 1927. The earthquake brought death to about five hundred people. There were further three hundred and fifty-two seriously wounded to the west of the Jordan, and three hundred and sixty-two to the east. In Jerusalem one hundred and seventy-five houses were destroyed.[3] How an earthquake is felt is seen from Isa. 13.7-8: 'Therefore shall all hands be feeble, and every heart of man shall melt. They shall be dismayed. Pangs and sorrows shall take hold of them. They shall be in pain, as a woman in travail. They shall look at one another amazed.' These earthquakes come over

[1] For the correct interpretation of Ps. 72.7 'till the moon be no more' cf. L. Köhler, *Kleine Lichter* (1945), pp. 57 ff.

[2] In the letter of James, this becomes three years and six months (5.17), probably in order to fit this period into the apocalyptic system which reckons in sevens.

[3] F.-M. Abel, *Géographie de la Palestine*, II (second edition 1933), pp. 33 ff.: 'Les tremblements de terre.'

and over again, sometimes weaker, sometimes more violent. Everyone experiences them, and everyone has felt the terror of them. In our time, those of our contemporaries who have lived through bombardment and continually repeated air-raid alarms may again get rest, but the terror remains hidden in them, and who can say when they will be really free from it? In the same way, the Hebrew lived with a feeling of insecurity. We can appreciate the dating of the words of Amos 'two years before the earthquake' (Amos 1.1), even though historians and critics find it inadequate. We may appreciate still more why the Bible speaks of falling mountains and collapsing hills. Such things really happened, and if a man has experienced it, where can he find security?

The Greeks had for the world the word '*kosmos*'. By Greeks we here mean that small, exalted stratum which is always referred to when we speak of the Greeks, not the Greek people as a whole, of whom we know practically nothing, because the scholars just ignore them as if they were not there. '*Kosmos*' means 'ornament', 'beautiful order'. To the Greeks the world is like a tidy room in which everything is in its right place, and to discover and set out these right places and their reasonable relationship to one another was what the Greek mind—the most inquisitive and most eager for knowledge—set out to do from an early time, and it found marvellous and reasonable answers to many of its questions. All of us, and all our science and technology, would be desperately impoverished had the Greeks not done this.

The Romans called the world *natura*, nature, that is what is born, what grows, what happens. Everything which has come into being is as it is because it has come into being. What more need one ask? The Roman is no Greek. But what the Greeks discovered and elaborated, the Romans were able to spread abroad in the world by their power and by their language. The Hebrew, if he has any name at all for the world, calls it '*ōlām*. What this word means cannot be said with any certainty. Probably it means something hidden, unknown, mysterious. But even if this meaning is wrong, it would be very fitting. For to the Hebrew the whole world is a mystery. He neither understands it, nor does he penetrate it and examine it. He is no Greek. It is not a matter of chance, but quite in accord with his nature, that the Hebrew has hardly any abstract terms, hardly any general concepts.[1] He takes things as they are, as he himself sees them. He accepts them, and marvels. The question is which things—material and immaterial—fall within his purview. Any man who tried to be aware of all the objects and facts which fall upon his senses and his mind, who tried to absorb and consider them all, would be overwhelmed by the mass of them. We all make selections. The farmer calls the plants which have no value for him 'weeds', and dismisses them thus. He does not know the names of the mountains around him, because he does not climb them. If we look at the classification of the animals and plants in the first creation narrative, we see the simplification, indeed the poverty of the selection. Under the one term 'green things' there are two kinds of plants, those which only last for a year ('*ēṣeb*), and those which are perennial ('*ēṣ*) and among the animals

[1] Lazar Gülkowitsch, *Die Bildung von Abstraktbegriffen in der hebräischen Sprachgeschichte* (1931).

there are the domesticated animals (bĕhēmāh) and the wild animals (ḥayyath hā'āreṣ), and further the creeping things (remeṣ), the winged creatures ('ōph), the swarming things which swarm in the waters (shereṣ), and the great sea-monsters (tannīn) (Gen. 1.11-25). Only in Job, which really is almost a learned work, do we find a more detailed naming and description. The urge to collect, to sift, to recognize is not strong. We have only to compare this with Aristotle and Pliny to see the difference.

So if a man comes across a creature, or some other phenomenon or event which is not familiar and not known by name, what happens? For this the Hebrew has the word *pele'* and its derivatives. That is a 'miracle'. Miracles among the Hebrews are, however, not wonders in the theological or scholastic sense—or at least not that alone. In this more limited sense they are divided into three stages: the interruption of the natural order—that is really a Greek philosophical contribution—the miracle itself, and then the restoration of the normal course of nature. Miracles of this kind are also known to the Hebrew. How should he not know of them? He relates them and honours them as revelations and mighty acts, *gebūrōth* (the ἀρεταί of I Pet. 2.9) of God. But as our words 'wonder' and 'to wonder' have a wider meaning, so also do the Greek terms θαῦμα, θαυμάζειν. The Latin *miraculum* really means 'that which is observed carefully' because it is unexpected, or unaccustomed. So it is, too, with the Hebrew words and concepts which are used in such contexts. Everything which goes beyond the normal everyday experience; everything which strikes the Hebrew as astonishing or unexpected—all that is miracle. He lives thus in a world of continuous miracle. Miracles meet him at every step.

The question is how he regards these miracles and in what way they affect his feeling about life. When Moses as shepherd of Jethro was driving his flocks over the grassy steppes, he came to the mount of God without knowing it, and saw a bush which was in flames without being consumed. He decided to examine the thing more closely. 'I will turn aside now, and see this great sight. Why is the bush not burnt?' (Ex. 3.1-3). Would every Hebrew behave thus, or is it a result of Moses' special greatness that he so acts? The latter is more probable. For as a rule the Hebrew is alarmed by the unexpected. The words for terror and being terrified are various in the Old Testament and occur frequently. Even the shepherds in the field on the night of the nativity had to be told by the angel: 'Be not afraid' (Luke 2.10). It would be better to translate: 'Be not terrified'. For terror is not quite the same as fear. Fear is directed to a particular danger. Terror and awe do not come from a definite danger, which a man thinks he sees, but are the expression of something indefinite which makes a man feel insecure. Something has happened or has appeared which makes a man uncertain how he ought to conduct himself. This uncertainty fills the Hebrew in the face of the unexpected and unaccustomed. For this reason he avoids it when he can.

To this is added another factor, further to the uncertainty which always slumbers in the soul of the Hebrew and is ready to envelop him in anxiety. The world is sinister. Not only do the ever-threatening chaos, and the earthquakes, and the accidents of the course of nature make it sinister, but there is also another thing whose dark shadows fall only occasionally upon the pages of the Old Testament. This is the world of phantoms, of evil spirits and demons. We must not be deceived by the fact that they are, comparatively speaking, rarely mentioned in the Old Testament. Men do not speak willingly of them at all. Even our Swiss mountain-dwellers, who believe that they not infrequently have to contend with such beings, do not speak of them willingly. Who would speak willingly of the sinister? It could be invoked by speaking of it. The scriptures, moreover, with their faith in Yahweh, deny, if not the reality, at least the power of such beings, but to the mind of the Hebrew they are present and real.

In the earliest time, it is the giants (as the Greek Bible renders it), the *něphīlīm* (Gen. 6.4, Num. 13.33), which, as the name shows, are the creatures of terror which proceed from miscarriages. There is the presence of the 'sting' which goes around at midday (Ps. 91.6), a sort of dangerous Pan, whose time of activity is in the heat of the sun at its highest point, perhaps a personification of the fever and discomfort which makes itself felt in the hour of the day's greatest heat. There are the 'black ones' (Deut. 32.17, Ps. 106.37) to which unlawful sacrifices, even child sacrifices, were offered, to appease their evil will. There are the 'hairy-ones', the goat-spirits, which carry out their dances (Isa. 13.21). It may happen to a man to be witness of their crying one to another (Isa. 34.14). To them, too, sacrifices were offered in the cultic orgies (Lev. 17.7), and Jeroboam especially is said to have offered worship to them (II Chron. 11.15). There are the 'dry·ones', the demons of waterless places (Isa. 13.21, 23.13, 34.14, Jer. 50.39). There is Lilith (Isa. 34.14) and other demons. We must not imagine that their whole number is exhausted in the small amount of information which has come down to us.

If we ask whence belief in them and fear of them come, we must answer that the Hebrews have probably taken these over from the Canaanites. The desert, too, from which the Hebrew came, was not free of terrors, sinister things, voices in the night and other ghostly impressions. Canaanite gods were degraded to be demons and spirits, whose public worship or even the recognition of whose existence was officially forbidden. Yet they by no means died out in the secret consciousness of the people, and re-emerged at times to be once again vividly experienced and feared. Such a process has its parallels wherever a higher religion has driven out a lower.

The question as to where these evil spirits lived in popular belief takes us a considerable stage further. According to Isa. 13.20 ff. Babylon was destroyed and never inhabited again, but became a dwelling for hostile spirits. The ruins of houses and settlements were the dwellings of these spirits. There it was sinister, and this applied not only to Babylon, but to every place where men were once at home, and now only ruins and fragments of walls indicated their existence. There now were to be found sinister animals, for animals too with their howling, whining voices, their sudden springing up when anyone comes near them, are sinister. Men go quickly past, whistling and waving their hands to drive them away, or to hold them off, two clear signs of fear (Zeph. 2.13 ff., I Kings

9.8, Lam. 2.15, Jer. 19.8). Such a settlement or town or dwelling was cursed, and there is no doubt that there were many such places. Beware lest you approach them!

So there lay always over the whole land a clearly marked division between places which were safe and places which were haunted. It is safe where others go, where you go together, where men are to be met. Fields and pastures are places which evoke no anxiety. What lies beyond should be avoided. The Hebrew has no love of isolation. He does not wish to be alone and to wander off into the unknown.

It was Jesus who first made a decisive change in this, and the passages in which it is related of him have perhaps not been fully appreciated. 'In the morning, a great while before day, he rose up and went out and departed into a solitary place and there prayed' (Mark 1.35). It is several times related that Jesus sought loneliness. Jesus feared neither the dark nor isolation. He acknowledged no hostile spirits or ghosts, and so he gave men a freedom of which the Hebrew as yet knew nothing, for he was still bound.

This bondage surrounds the Hebrew's spirit on every side. He is bound by the expectation of a world catastrophe, as chaos takes away the foundation of his existence from under his feet. He is bound by the uncertainty as to whether to-morrow will dawn, or whether summer and harvest will come again next year. He is held by the indefinite, secret fear which earthquake and landslide have given him. He is oppressed by the puzzles of nature from which something unexpected or terrifying can come again and again—puzzles which he does not understand, which he does not examine, and in the face of which he never knows just how he ought to conduct himself. He is filled with a dark belief in demons and uncanny powers, whose activities he thinks he can detect in his illnesses, in the changes of his moods and the disturbances of his mind, in all the trials and afflictions which come unexplained upon him. For the Hebrew the word of Christ is certainly apt: 'In the world ye have tribulation' ($\theta\lambda\hat{\iota}\psi\iota\varsigma$ John 16.33).

What shall a man do in this tribulation? Just as a man who is caught by a violent storm unprotected in the open, crouches, draws in his head and shoulders, and waits in anxiety to see what will happen—for what else can he do?—so, one might say, does the Hebrew spirit react. The Hebrew withdraws into himself. He is not gifted with a desire for power, nor for a shaping of the world so that he is safe in it; he has no Promethean self-confidence. He has just a trustful patience and endurance, and above all shyness of anything new, of any daring, or of any change. The Hebrew depends upon tradition. He holds to what has been handed down. A man learns from his fathers and ancestors what he should do. As they acted, so he will act also. To deviate from tradition would be too greatly daring. It would almost be impiety and presumption.

This leaning towards tradition is carried through every department of Hebrew life, and the historian will immediately add by way of comment that this is what has preserved the Hebrew way of life, and is at the same time the great gift which Israel had to give to mankind in the providence of God, and which it still gives to-day by the absorption spiritually of the

Israelite deposit of thoughts and values in Christianity.

This clinging to tradition is clearly seen if we look at the technical aspect of Hebrew civilization. Scarcely any traces can be found of alterations in designs and processes—except perhaps in pottery—at least so far as we have knowledge of them. The same is true of agriculture, always the chief occupation of the Hebrew. 'His God doth instruct him aright, and doth teach him'; 'This also cometh forth from Yahweh of hosts, his counsel is wonderful and his wisdom is great' (Isa. 28.26, 29). If we turn to the constitution of the community—in the non-technical sense—even there only small alterations can be observed in the course of the centuries. Even in the mental sphere the changes are not great. This is one of the reasons why, in the same book, old and new writings, which came into existence over almost a thousand years, could be gathered together. The community of attitude and way of thought is stronger than the differences of time.

Here we meet with an outstanding characteristic of the Hebrew spirit. The matters to which he directs his attention are indeed very much the processes and movements of history. But the conception of history itself hardly plays any noticeable part. History presupposes the past, and what is past is what has lost its reality. In this sense the Hebrew mind hardly knows the past or history. The promises to the patriarchs are regarded by the later generations as valid for them still (though this word 'still' is not really appropriate). The Exodus from Egypt is not related at each Passover to no purpose. 'It shall be a sign unto thee upon thine hand, and for a memorial between thine eyes . . . for with a strong hand hath Yahweh brought thee out of

Egypt' (Ex. 13.9). What happened once is not a 'once' but a 'now'. It is 'we ourselves' whom he has brought out (Ex. 13.16). Past and present are one single act of God. The Exodus from Egypt and the return from Babylon are a single act of God delivering his people (Isa. 51.9-11). It is hardly comprehensible to-day that the Hebrew still experienced after centuries what had once happened. For the Hebrew mind this release from the past and from history was a living reality which creates life. It may well be because of this that the names of those who compiled the writings of the Old Testament are almost all unknown, and that we know practically nothing even about the great prophets. What do they matter to a mind which does not ask about the past?

This adherence to tradition naturally expresses itself most strongly, however, where it does also among other peoples and in other cultures, that is to say in the ordering of everyday life, and in the legal regulation of common life. Here too it has the most far-reaching consequences for the mental life of the Hebrew.

In everyday life the Hebrew does what he sees his fathers do. The modes of speech which he hears from them he uses also. The behaviour which he sees in them, he himself also follows. He carries out the details of his work as he sees them carry them out. He goes to the field and the pasture along their pathways, and must have very good reason for departing from them or for daring to go beyond them. For who knows what may be met with outside the well-trodden, old-established pathways? Outwardly and inwardly men go 'in the way of good men, and keep the paths of the righteous' (Prov. 2.20). Even the daughter of Lot in her audacious conduct appeals to the fact that there is no one there who can act 'after the manner of all the earth' (Gen. 19.31). Abimelech of Gerar reproaches Abraham, however, that he has treated him in a manner in which men ought not to behave (Gen. 20.9). Thus there are things which one does because the whole world does them, and there are things which one does not do because no one does them. That is tradition. Abraham explains his reasons. Tradition is valid where God is honoured. Since he did not believe that the people of Gerar would hold to this, he gave out that his wife was his sister (Gen. 20.11). Where tradition is firm and is respected by all, everything follows automatically, and there is no need of commands or of long explanations.

This firmly-established validity of tradition expresses itself also in the laws which have come down to us. It must strike the reader that the oldest collection, the so-called Book of the Covenant (Ex. 20.24-23.12, as it is normally delineated), contains definite and detailed prescriptions for many points of the common life, but that it does not touch on other departments of life at all. The same is true of that collection of laws[1] from the seventh century which we call Deuteronomy. Two things are lacking in this collection, which has continued to exercise such great influence even down to

---

[1] The difference between a law book and a collection of laws is often missed, but is of fundamental importance. A law book represents the ordering of the common life according to far-reaching principles and with the aim of laying down laws. A collection of laws is a gathering together of ancient and newer laws, in which the aim of laying down law is not indeed lacking, but the unified underlying conception is missing. It was thus that Deuteronomy was formed. Cf. also Appendix, p. 170 n. 1.

our own time: it is not comprehensive in its regulations, nor is it unified in the principles of its selection. Rather do its contents make a strong impression of haphazard arrangement. The reason for this is no doubt the same as in the Book of the Covenant. Only those regulations are taken up which, at the time of its publication, needed a particular reminder and stress. the remainder is covered by tradition. When tradition is sufficiently alive and clear, there is no need for legal regulation.

A third collection of laws and precepts leads us a stage further in the description of the mental life of the Hebrew. These are the legal requirements which are counted as part of the priestly code. They are not completely unified, but they have one place of origin: the exile. It is characteristic of them that they—in common with the two books of law already mentioned —are traced back to Moses without any attempt at dealing with the historical facts. This is not a mere literary fiction, but expresses the strength of the idea of tradition. What to-day is proper, was always so. What is law derives from Moses, the man of God (Ps. 90 title [Heb. v. 1]), who was the real giver of law and order to the people of Israel. History there certainly is, in the sense that God helped the people of God also in the time of their forefathers. But contemporaries and forefathers are one unity. History as a time division is not known.

The legal requirements which are reckoned to the priestly code belong in this connection for two quite different reasons. They go back to Ezekiel, the real 'father of Judaism', and his circle. Their goal is the preservation in spiritual matters of the Jewish religious community in the scattering of the exile. The community can be held together by giving it firm rules. What was formerly tradition now becomes law, contained in strict regulations. Thus we get the laws of the sabbath, the distinction of clean and unclean, particularly of foods, and other such matters. The consequence of this regulating is the growth of an ever more carefully worked out casuistry, that is the meticulous distinction of what is allowed and when it is allowed, and what is not allowed and when not. The consequence is that it must be known what sin is. Sin is what is forbidden. But the knowledge of what is forbidden and what is not is, in fact, unlimited. Distinctions can be made more and more finely, and even with the best will in the world it is possible for a man sometimes to overlook or not to know what is not permitted. So in the individual action or abstention, it is no longer the moral will which decides, as was still possible under the rule of tradition, but more and more 'knowledge'. It is possible to act unintentionally in a way that is not permitted, and so the position arises more and more that one acts or abstains because it is commanded or forbidden, without any longer realizing why it should be the one or the other. The free moral will recedes into the background. The anxiety to act rightly, and even more the anxiety not to act wrongly, press into the forefront of behaviour. There comes into being a religion of anxiety, which brings with it the psychoses and neuroses which are so often to be found in later Judaism (cf. p. 19).

But the other point which must here be noted is this. The priestly code, together with the laws which are to be reckoned to it, is a great presentation of history. It begins with the creation, and runs through the revelation to Abraham to the revelation to Moses, and the proclamation of the law of God by Moses. The remainder is the fulfilment of the promise to Abraham, the taking of the promised land.[1] And what then?

The promises go no further. The land of Canaan is from now on Israel's 'everlasting possession' (Gen. 17.8). The people of Israel live there under the 'everlasting covenant' (Gen. 17.7) with God. They are his people, he is their God (Ex. 6.7). Neither in space nor time can there be anything else or anything new. Nothing further in space, because Israel does not desire anything beyond its borders. The world-view which opens up in the prophets—all nations will come up to the mountain of Yahweh, that he may teach us his ways and we may walk in his paths (Isa. 2.3), that from the rising of the sun to the going down of the same Yahweh's name may be great among the nations (Mal. 1.11)—this aspect of the world-mission is nowhere to be found in the priestly code. Nor does it contain anything of an outlook into the future in time.[2] This is not a matter of chance, but quite deliberate. Israel, the people of the revealed God, with its worship of this one and only God, ordained once and for all by what was given by God himself through Moses—Israel is a world to itself. It is the community of God, in the

[1] This term 'Landnahme' (taking of the land), which is especially well-chosen and valuable for research, we owe to A. Alt, 'Die Landnahme der Israeliten in Palästina' (1925) E. T. in Essays (1966), pp. 133-169.
[2] At best one could point to the chronology discussed in the note on p. 41, whose figures may have been adapted as time went on, and perhaps originally pointed to the period after 500, approximately the time of the priestly code. But this chronological aim is never clearly expressed.

world but not of the world, in time but not of time. Israel's only duty, the only reason for its existence, is the right worship of God, as it ought to have been observed from the fathers onwards. This is the supreme expression of the power of tradition over the spirit of the Hebrew.

The strength of tradition takes on just in this connection a significance for the whole of history, and one which even touches us, and with this we come to the end of what can here be said of the mental life of the Hebrew. During the whole of their historical existence the Hebrews lived within the orbit of the influence of foreign nations and great cultures. There were the Egyptians, who over and over again extended their power from the delta towards the north, and, as the Tell el-Amarna letters show, occupied many places in Palestine. Their intellectual influence on the Hebrews was amazingly small. There was the Assyro-Babylonian culture, much closer to the Hebrews in language and probably also in make-up. At the time when the texts of this culture were deciphered, research was under the influence of the idea that anything among the Hebrews which even vaguely corresponded to some scrap of Accadian material, or seemed to correspond, showed the influence of the great culture upon this small people. But we have long recognized that forms of words, even when they extend to whole idioms, do not tell us very much; for every idiom and form of speech is part and parcel of a cultural whole and can only be understood and used to form a proper judgment if it is considered in the context of its place of origin. Intellectual properties, even the smallest, cannot just be interchanged like the screws and rods of two machines. There is no doubt that the Assyro-Babylonian culture, much more than the Egyptian, provided the basis for almost all the cultural outlook of the Near East. But on a common soil plants of quite different kinds may grow, and the soil is for the plant only one of many conditions which determine its growth and form.

The same is true to-day of Ugaritic. We are only at the beginning of our knowledge of it, and however bold many of the translators and interpreters are—and we are not disputing their great services—it is quite certain that in a short time we shall know many things more accurately, and regard them differently. Even so the remarkable fact can already to-day be seen that the Ugaritic writings and the Ugaritic thought contained in them are full of myths of which there is scarcely a trace in Hebrew thought. Ugaritic thought is the expression of a highly developed urban culture, whereas Hebrew is rooted entirely in the land. We cannot yet say how far Ugaritic—viewed as a culture—stands in the context and under the influence of neighbouring urban cultures such as the Babylonian. Hebrew thought—even when viewed as a cultural form—was able to protect itself from Babylonian. Even in the time when the Babylonian threat was greatest, the time of the Babylonian exile, the conscious monotheism of Deutero-Isaiah breaks through as a rejection of the Babylonian Pantheon, and as a victory over it, and remained valid for all the following period. In the struggle, a heroic spiritual struggle, the Hebrew tradition asserted itself. It asserted itself and struggled through, rejecting and struggling, to the final clarity of its understanding of God.

This did not happen without an earlier spiritual struggle, which was equally dangerous and much more wearisome and long-drawn-out. Hebrew tradition was threatened by Canaanite Baalism, was half consumed by it, and yet came out as master. The clearest witness to this struggle and to the decisive rejection of Baalism is the message of Hosea. 'It shall be at that day, saith Yahweh, that she (the woman Israel) shall call me "my spouse" (*'īshī*) and no longer "my husband" (*ba'ǎlī*). For I will take away the names of the Baalim out of her mouth, and they shall no more be mentioned by their name' (Hos. 2.16 f. [Heb. 18 f.]). Two words representing two different worlds—on the one hand sensuality, on the other ethic.

If we ask what is the basis of this ethic, this decision in favour of making a contrast between good and evil, we come upon the basic form of Hebrew community life, the community of law, and upon the basic type of human relationship in which the fundamental characteristic of the Hebrew's mental make-up is revealed. This is the fact that in Hebrew community life one point decides the issue, namely that each man should give the other his rights. The profoundest content of the tradition, of the ordering of practice, law and custom, is righteousness. The individual Hebrew lives with his neighbour and his companions in the village on the basis of a mutual recognition and of simple, righteous settlement of opposing claims and rights. All are free citizens. This is revealed by the way in which they speak with one another and with their king. But one bright star shines over these free citizens—righteousness. If righteousness is injured, then the orderliness of life is disturbed. Then the prophets speak of judgment, and they speak as messengers of God, for God himself desires righteousness.

God reveals himself to peoples in the concepts and ways of thought which are natural to them. This is what Jesus means when he says that those will see God who are pure in heart (Matt. 5.8). Just because the Hebrew in his life with his fellows is intent on seeing that everything happens in a righteous settlement, Israel can hear the message that God desires righteousness. There is something more here than is found in Egypt and Babylon and Ugarit. Here is a people to which it is granted to see the holiness of God. Here is a people which, however small and unimportant it might seem to other nations, was called and chosen to proclaim in all the world the message of the God who will speak justice between the nations and will reprove many peoples (Isa. 2.4).

Thus the unknown composer of the Old Testament proverbs cries: 'Righteousness exalteth a nation' (Prov. 14.34), and the New Testament apostle replies: 'The kingdom of God is righteousness and peace and joy in the Holy Spirit' (Rom. 14.17).

8

APPENDIX

JUSTICE IN THE GATE

RECTORIAL Address given at the ninety-eighth anniversary of the foundation of the University of Zürich, 29 April, 1931.

I

It is often forgotten that the scene of the biblical events is a land of mountains. Hebron lies 3,040 feet above sea level, Jerusalem on average about 2,500, Samaria 1,454, and even Nazareth 1,148. Further, the Mediterranean coast is only about twenty to thirty-five miles from these places, and the Jordan valley, which lies some hundreds of feet below sea level, is only about eighteen to twenty-two miles away, as the crow flies, with the result that the many valleys to east and west of the water-shed cut sharply down from the upper levels of the land. It is therefore no wonder that it has been reckoned that there are more than forty natural divisions of Palestine.[1] These are, moreover, so sharply divided from one another that even a modern state with its unifying forces of road-building, administration, education and economic co-ordination would have difficulty in overcoming their natural separateness.

[1] Valentin Schwöbel, *Die Landesnatur Palästinas*, Part 2 (1914), p. 52.

Such a state, with its power and administration, did not exist in antiquity. After the invasion by the Hebrews, Palestine was at first, as has recently been well demonstrated,[1] a kind of confederacy, whose delegates came together for consultation once or twice in the year at one of the great sanctuaries. The kingdom established by Saul and David was more a community created by necessity than a living unity, being more effective in war than in peace, and already at the death of Solomon it fell apart into two states. Even in this dual form, the parts were not really more strongly unified than before. To the end there was only a framework, and not a pattern which really bound together all the members into one whole.

Thus from the beginning right down till nearly the end of the period, the community life of Palestine depended upon the separate natural divisions of the country. Each one lived on its own resources, and lived to itself. It shaped its own life according to the special needs and laws of its position. The achievement of unity in spite of this depended on the fact that in the individual districts the same conditions and activities led to the same patterns, rather than that there was a unified will of a political kind which worked upon them.

But if we ask what was the strongest force making for community life in the districts, there can be no doubt of the answer. It was law. Community life depends entirely upon peace, that is a state of affairs in which the members of the community have their

---

[1] Martin Noth, *Das System der zwölf Stämme Israels* (1930), appropriately introduces the concept of an 'ancient Israelite amphictyony'. Cf. also Albrecht Alt, *Die Staatenbildung der Israeliten in Palästina* (1930), pp. 10 ff. E. T. in *Essays* (1966), pp. 171-237, esp. 179 ff.

claims and needs fairly adjusted to one another. The one force which makes for this peace and preserves it is law. Law is sacred, because it is the guarantee of community life. The community has no more precious possession and no more lively concern than law. In preserving it and exercising it, the community is alive, and really expresses itself. How true this was in the Hebrew countryside may be best seen in the way in which men gathered in the legal assembly—in the formation, history, and working of this system.

The book of Ruth tells (4.1-2) of the summoning of such an assembly for law. A citizen of Bethlehem is concerning himself with the family rights and inheritance of two widows. In the early morning, before any of the citizens of the place have yet gone out to work in the fields, he goes to the gate through which they must all pass, and sits down there. He calls the person who is most nearly affected by this legal matter, and calls further ten other citizens to the legal discussion, and sets out the matter, which is then treated in the proper legal manner. When, many years ago, I pointed out the archaeological interest of this passage,[1] Georg Cohn here in Zürich and Josef Kohler in Berlin, two men to whom the history of law is in so many ways indebted, both drew my attention to the similar 'street law' in Schwyz, Nidwalden and Appenzell. The existence of this had been pointed out by Eduard Osenbrüggen, who was also formerly in Zürich.[2] The historian and the ethnologist who are concerned with law will of course be able to point to a host of related

[1] Z.A.W., xxxiv (1914), p. 146.
[2] Z.A.W., xxxvi (1916), p. 21. Eduard Osenbrüggen, *Studien zur deutschen und schweizerischen Rechtsgeschichte* (1868), pp. 58-65.

phenomena and practices. The historian of law will also immediately realize that the ten legal assessors in Ruth are none other than a commission representing the whole of the citizens who are capable of administering law. A number of such points of interest can be noted.

We will not, however, stop to elaborate this, but go on immediately to attempt to describe the institution of the Hebrew legal assembly in its main features. Each district of Palestine contains a number of places, which are all independent settlements. The relationship of these places to one another varies. To some extent it may be that of a 'mother' village to its offshoots.[1] For since the inhabitants of a Hebrew village are all of them peasants, the settlement cannot grow beyond a certain size. A peasant village must never grow beyond the limit within which it is possible for all the peasants to get out to their daily work in the field in a reasonable space of time. As soon as this limit is passed, part of the population must move away and found a branch or colony on new territory. To some extent also the settlements of the same district may be quite independent of one another, self-contained within their own community life. The nature of the legal assembly demands that each place should normally form its own body for purposes of legal action.

The population of each place consists of two groups, at least as far as our present purpose is concerned. One group is composed of the full citizens, the other of the remainder of the inhabitants—women, children, slaves, and the 'stranger that is within thy gates', that is immigrants, who for reasons of blood feud, outlawry

[1] The Hebrew word for a branch village is *bath*, 'daughter'. (cf. p. 70).

or for some other cause do not live in the place in which they are full citizens. Full citizens are those men who occupy their own property, who do not stand under any kind of tutelage, and can claim the four great rights—marriage, cult, war and the administration of law. Among these, the right to marriage is for the Hebrew something almost essential, that of war is an exception, that of the cult is something occasional, its responsibility felt no doubt more than its enjoyment. The supreme right, in which is experienced the pride and worth of a healthy man, who is of age, has his own property and is recognized by his fellows, is the right to take part and to speak in the legal assembly. It is the meeting place of those who really matter.

The legal assembly carries out its functions in the gate. The prophets repeatedly warned men that righteousness should dwell in the gates. What is meant is the gate of the settlement,[1] the only entrance and exit of the protected area. Since all are peasants, all may be met here in the early morning. 'The Lord keep thy going out and thy coming in' runs the blessing (Ps. 121.8). We should say 'going in and out' because we think of the coming and going of a guest, or of someone occupying a house. But the Hebrew places 'going out' before 'coming in', for he is thinking of the going out of the peasant to his fields in the morning, and of his return thence in the evening.[2] For this reason the legal assembly meets in the morning ('soberly in the morning' as it is laid down in the regulation of the

[1] Against Sigmund Mowinckel, 'I porten', in *Studier tilegnede Frants Buhl . . . af fagfaeller og elever* (1925), pp. 167-180.
[2] Ludwig Köhler, 'Der Tageslauf des Hebräers', in *Festschrift für Paul W. Schmiedel, Protestantische Monatshefte* (1921), pp 237 f.

Appenzell 'street court' of 1585). The word 'soberly' might appear to suggest the reason for this regulation—though, as I think, wrongly. For though this might be appropriate for the men of Appenzell, it is not the reason for the time of meeting among the Hebrews. The reason is rather the one that has already been mentioned. From this we may understand expressions like the lovely word of praise: 'Every morning Yahweh dispenses his justice' (Zeph. 3.5). In the freshness of the morning, in the light of day, there will be found judgment, clear and shining.

The legal assembly comes together when there is need. In one instance we can see vividly how it is conducted. The prophet Jeremiah has gone up into the temple court and has committed the enormity of pronouncing for the temple of Jerusalem a downfall in ruins, and Jerusalem's own destruction as an example of Yahweh's curse. Priests, prophets and all sorts of people heard this, and he has hardly finished before they rush upon him with the cry: 'Thou art worthy of death'. The leading men of the district, who hear the uproar, come in haste and immediately the scene becomes a tribunal. The leading men sit down in the gate, the priests and prophets make their complaints, and Jeremiah carries on his defence, less wordily but not with less dignity than Socrates in the *Apology* of Plato. Then the leading men and the assembled people give judgment: 'This man is not worthy of death' (Jer. 26). A process of judgment in its proper forms has here taken place. Called into being in a moment, it immediately concludes the affair. It will always have been like this in the petty affairs of the smaller places, and in any case we have no information anywhere of

JUSTICE IN THE GATE

regular days for court sessions, nor of times when the law courts were not in session. If two citizens or families or other groups have a legal dispute, or if a crime or misdeed has been committed, then whoever desires judgment calls for it, and all willingly respond to the call, for the administration of justice is the affair of everyone. It is also the delight of all, as the modern countryman may still realize, and even the modern town-dweller may be just aware of it.

Of the special customs observed on these occasions we know only the one that the assessors sit down to administer law. 'Sit ye down here. And they sat down' is how it runs in Ruth (4.2). When a man speaks, he stands up. From the expression 'The wicked may not stand in the legal assembly' (Ps. 1.5. R.V. 'shall not stand in the judgment'), I once thought we should conclude that the accused waited during the discussion of his guilt kneeling or lying on the ground. But this is not certain.[1]

What is the purpose of the legal assembly when it meets? It has come into existence as the result of something which happens wherever groups of men are formed for continuous life together. We must go back to this if we are to understand the inmost purpose of the legal assembly and the ideas which always underlie its decisions. If within a group which has some continuous existence the inclinations, wishes, desires or actions of two individuals come into conflict, then such a conflict may for a long time remain their own concern, one which they can settle for themselves unaided, either by words or by blows. But there comes

---

[1] 'Eine Rechtssitte in einem Eigennamen.' Z.A.W., xxxvi (1916), pp. 27 f.

a point when such a conflict of two members of the group disturbs the well-being of the group itself. The group is disturbed, irritated by the quarrel, and even in some circumstances its existence is endangered. Then it intervenes, and makes the quarrel its own affair, and settles it in order to be free of the danger, and settles it in such a way as to accommodate the desires of all parties as far as is possible. This intervention, on such grounds and for such purposes, is the duty of the legal assembly. It is the organization for reconciliation. It grows up out of a practical need. It does not go beyond this in its actions nor in its outlooks. It intervenes when it must, but does not intervene any further than it must. It has no desire to provide systematic law. Nor does it act in systematic legal ways, but its sole endeavour is to settle quarrels and to guard the well-being of the community. To judge means here to settle. The saying '*Fiat justitia, pereat mundus*'—we need not here discuss what value, if any, can be given to such a statement—is not only unknown to the Hebrew legal assembly, it would be incomprehensible, and would in fact be rejected by that assembly if it were ever heard. It is important to realize accurately this attitude of the Hebrew legal assembly. For only so can one understand why the bases and methods of its action have always remained primitive.

All who have legal rights are judges, and this activity of judgment is understood to be that of giving assistance to justice. To judge does not mean establishing the facts of a criminal offence and then judging and sentencing on the basis of this establishment of fact, but, in Hebrew, 'to judge' and 'to help' are parallel ideas.

'Judge the fatherless' says the prophet (Isa. 1.17). This does not mean 'condemn him', but 'help him to his rights'. 'Judge me, O God' is on four occasions the prayer of the Psalmist (7.8 [Heb. 9], 26.1, 35.24, 43.1). It is not the prayer of the guilty for his punishment, but the cry of the persecuted for help in the gaining of justice. This correct statement of the linguistic evidence[1] explains why the characters who free the Israelite tribes and groups of tribes from foreign domination in the period before the monarchy are called 'judges'. They are not men who pronounce judgment, but 'helpers', war being here regarded as the means by which right is achieved.

Judges and witnesses are therefore not differentiated. The same man may in the same case and at the same assembly for judgment be addressed as witness and as judge. Actual legal standards, particularly such as are tied to formulae, are lacking. At most the legal assembly will have in mind certain earlier decisions as precedents, as did in fact happen in the proceedings against Jeremiah (Jer. 26.17-19). Indeed, the writing down of the laws—a matter into which we have not

[1] This fact is not recognized by H. W. Hertzberg, 'Die Entwicklung des Begriffes *mischpat* im Alten Testament', Z.A.W., xl (1922), pp. 256-287. One can indeed say that it is completely misunderstood. Hertzberg thinks that the original meaning of *shāphat* was 'to rule' and that *mishpāt* originally meant something like 'persistent firmness in action' (p. 263). But on this assumption it is not possible to explain satisfactorily either the one hundred and eighty-five occurrences of the verb, or the four hundred and twenty-six of the noun. *Shāphat* originally means 'to decide between', *mishpāt* means in most cases 'a decision which is valid for a person'. From this can be derived quite naturally the two most common meanings, 'a legal decision, judgment' and 'a legal claim which someone has' (legal claim—cf. the right of the king I Sam. 8.9, of daughters Ex. 21.9, of priests over against people I Sam. 2.13). That it could easily develop from this into the meaning 'duty' (I Kings 4.28 [Heb. 5.8]) or 'custom rule' (18.28), can readily be seen.

here time to go—expresses certain laws just in that form of precedent.[1]

The proceedings of the legal assembly are almost exclusively oral, though not necessarily always so. As to the forms of the proceedings we have information concerning the basic methods and the individual turns of phrase in a writing whose significance as a source of this kind has not before been recognized. It is the book of Job. Here, in Chapters 3-31, we have a whole series of individual speeches, made by four speakers, who form two parties. Job sets out a statement, or, rather, he makes a complaint:

> 'Wherefore does God give light to him that is in misery
> And life unto the bitter in soul? . . .
> Who would rejoice exceedingly,
> And would be glad if they could find the grave' (3.20, 22).

A friend answers him, reproaching him and contradicting. Job speaks again, without showing himself convinced; a second and then a third friend interchange speech with him. This dialogue form is repeated a second time with all the speakers, and Job clearly here represents the one party while his three friends represent the opposition, and it is repeated even a third time, except that the third friend says nothing more here. Finally Job sums up in his last speech, which, especially in Chapter 31, surpasses all that has gone before in depth and passion.

It must be clearly and explicitly emphasized that in the few remarks which we are here making concerning

---

[1] Thus with regard to the question as to how the men of war and the camp-followers are to divide the spoil (I Sam. 30.21-25); or the question as to what rights of inheritance belong to the daughters of a man who dies without sons (Num. 27.1-11).

this part of the book of Job, the most important aspect, namely the significance of these chapters in their content and theology, cannot be discussed. It is just the formal aspect with which we are concerned here. For if we inquire from the expositors of the book of Job how this series of speeches is to be regarded, we find to our surprise an embarrassed silence, which is most unusual among theologians. They speak of a dialogue which these chapters are supposed to contain, and an exposition is not lacking which attempts to make a link between this supposed dialogue of the Bible and those of Plato.[1] But even Renan[2] had objected that there is no development of thought in Job as there is in Plato. Just as in the questions and rejoinders of the lawyer and his client, so here by Job on the one side and the three on the other side, essentially the same thing is being said over and over again. Gunkel, otherwise so noted and honoured for his determining of 'forms' of passages of Old Testament literature, speaks here, almost modestly, of 'disputations of the wise'.[3] Peters, one of the most recent and best exegetes of Job, says that it is 'a didactic dialogue for parenetic purposes'.[4] That too has more sound than meaning. Of one thing there can be no doubt at all. These speeches are speeches like those which were delivered by the parties before the legal assembly. They are 'party addresses'. The construction of them is decisive for this. Before the legal assembly the speech and counterspeech con-

[1] N. K. Fries, *Das philosophische Gespräch von Hiob bis Platon* (1904).
[2] Quoted in A. Kuenen, *Historisch-kritische Einleitung in die Bücher des Alten Testaments* Part 3, Section 1 (1894), p. 117.
[3] Article 'Hiob' in *Die Religion in Geschichte und Gegenwart* (second edition 1928), Vol. II, col. 1929.
[4] N. Peters, *Das Buch Hiob* (1928), p. 59*.

tinue back and forth until the one party has nothing more to say. For this reason the third friend finally speaks no more.

As soon as this is recognized, many things become clear; for example, the lack of real progress in the thought. The intention is not, as in a Platonic dialogue, to find truth in speech and counterspeech, but the presentation of a point of view already determined beforehand with such forcefulness as to persuade the listeners. Indeed one might well also say that it is to 'talk them round'. Job's last utterance is also to be understood similarly. With a forcefulness both of form and of content, with which one can compare little else, save perhaps parts of King Lear or Faust, Job presents the affirmation that he is innocent.

> 'If I have lifted up my hand against the fatherless,
> Because I saw my helpers in the gate, . . .
> Then let my arm be broken from its socket' (31.21 f.).

> 'If my step hath turned out of the way, . . .
> And if any spot hath cleaved to mine hands:
> Then let me sow, and let another eat;
> Yea, let the produce of my field be rooted out' (31.7 f.).

This is the conditional self-cursing of the accused, who thereby seeks to prove his innocence before the legal assembly.

> 'O, that I had one to hear me!
> Lo, here is my house sign,[1] let the Almighty answer me' (31.35).

[1] *Thāwī* is not easy to interpret. Budde (1913) 'my cross', from the shape of the letter: Steuernagel in Kautzsch (1923) 'my signature', in other words a Tau which represented a signature; König (1929) 'my signature mark'; Peters (1928) 'my mark', meaning 'the mark which

JUSTICE IN THE GATE 161

This is the effective close of the defence, which becomes a challenge. The same method is used throughout these chapters, in so far as the content does not suppress the forms which belong to the legal assembly. They are a treasury for the legal formulae and advocates' phrases of the Hebrews.

The opponent is shown a reflection of the kind of person that one could really expect him to be:

> 'The despairing deserves to be shown kindness by his friend,
> Even if he forsakes the fear of God the Almighty
> But my friends have shown themselves deceitful as a brook' (6.14 f.).

The opponent is challenged to speak something more to the point:

> 'Teach me, and I will hold my peace:
> And cause me to understand wherein I err!
> How forcible are words of uprightness!
> But what doth your arguing prove' (6.24 f.).

The opponent is seriously blamed for speaking so long and with so little content:

> 'How long wilt thou speak these things
> And the words of thy mouth come like a mighty wind?'
> (8.2).

He expresses moral indignation:

replaces a signature', in which there is a particular nicety since Job's fingers and hands were eaten away by leprosy. I should prefer to think of a *wasm*, as Musil, *Arabia Petraea*, Vol. III (1908), pp. 28, 30, 32 ff. illustrates them. The modern peasant too still has a 'house-sign' which he cuts into his tools to protect them from pilferers. The second half of v. 35 I regard as incomprehensible.

> 'Should a man full of words receive no answer?
> Should a man full of talk be justified?
> Should thy boasting make men hold their peace?
> And when thou mockest, shall no man make thee ashamed?' (11.2 f.).

He is mocked:

> 'No doubt but ye are the people,
> And wisdom shall die with you.
> But I have understanding as well as you' (12.2 f.)

Or:

> 'Should a wise man make answer with vain knowledge,
> And fill his belly with the east wind?
> Should he reason with unprofitable talk?
> Or with speeches wherewith he can do no good?' (15.2 f.).

The opponent is accused of triviality:

> 'I have heard many such things:
> Miserable comforters are ye all.
> Are vain words now at an end?
> Or what provoketh thee that thou answerest yet?
> I also could speak as ye do
> If I were in your place,
> I could join words together against you,
> And shake mine head at you' (16.2-4).

These examples are sufficient. We cannot here treat the whole of the material exhaustively, and anyone experienced in law will long have been observing that more than two thousand years ago the same arguments were clearly used as to-day. What we wished to demonstrate has, we hope, been attained. It is possible to reconstruct the approximate procedure of the legal assembly, and its influence is obvious on the formal language of the literature—a subject on which much more might well be said.[1]

Perhaps, before we turn to other matters, we should briefly answer two questions. First, the question concerning the influence of the priests on legal practice. It is apparently much less than we are tempted to assume on a first examination of the Old Testament. Since the priesthood is inherited, traditions concerning earlier decisions will naturally have been particularly strongly preserved in the priestly families, and as members of the legal assembly, as citizens not as priests, they took for this reason a lively and important part in its activities. But the picture which we normally get of the cultural conditions of the Hebrews is overlaid with cultic matters, because the Old Testament received its latest form not in the Hebrew state, but in the Jewish cult-community. Certainly there will have been cases where the legal assembly could not get any further by means of party discussions, the proving of witnesses, the establishing of guilt and the discovery of the right according to traditional rules or free decision. There then remained the last resort, that of allowing the oracle to decide, and its management was originally the main business of the priest. Then he would speak and exercise his influence. But we have little information concerning this, and we may guess that it was exceptional and seldom occurred.

A second question concerns the possibility of making an appeal from the local legal assembly to a higher authority. Here we are well informed. A widow came to David because her only two sons had

[1] Cf. on this L. Köhler, *Deuterojesaja stilkritisch untersucht* (1923), par. 83-87.

quarrelled so fiercely that the one had killed the other and so become a murderer. At this point the family of the dead father had intervened[1] and wished to carry out blood revenge on the murderer. But this would have as its consequence that the direct line of the dead husband of the woman would die right out, and, in order to prevent this, she brought the case to the king. Similarly we are told that Absalom betook himself in the early morning to the gate to intercept the Judahites who wished to bring their legal affairs to the king. So too the prophet Nathan came to David and laid a legal case before him.[2] It is thus possible to go against the legal assembly or even to go over its head to lay a matter before the king. Conversely, the king will have had the right to draw any particular legal case under his own jurisdiction if he wished to do so. In this a higher kind of legal court was being created. The conduct of law becomes the affair of the king. By a logical development it might have become the affair of the state, but this logical development never took place. There is no trace of higher legal rights being exercised by the king. Another type of development was followed instead, though this first possibility was known to the Hebrews, for when the people asked for a king, against the wishes of Samuel (the account is late and remote from the events), it is said: 'That we also may be like all the nations; and that our king may judge

[1] II Sam. 14.1 ff. The story shows in addition that in the time of David questions of blood revenge were still settled apart from the law, and not necessarily submitted to the legal assembly. Similarly, until the year 625 parents had the right to kill a rebellious son (Deut. 21.18-21). Only then did the disposal of his life become a matter for the decision of the legal assembly. This regulation, indeed, influenced Italian criminal law until modern times, and no doubt influenced other law as well. (Cf. also p. 109.)

[2] II Sam. 15.1-6 and 12.1 ff.

us, and go out before us, and fight our battles.' (I Sam. 8.20). The king is chief judge and army leader. In this he has forerunners, if the report is historical that Samuel and his sons travelled around in the land and gave judgment, no doubt as plenipotentiaries of the tribal group which is nowadays assumed as the state before the kingdom among the Hebrews.[1] But there is not much indication of such a higher court of law.

II

Thus for hundreds of years in the villages and countryside of Palestine the legal assembly met in the open air and administered justice. It rarely had to handle important matters. A right of way, rights to a well, a theft of someone else's cattle, an assault which had a serious sequel, a death by violence, a claim to an inheritance—these will have been the sort of questions with which the administrators of justice concerned themselves, and their labours were for a long time reduced by the fact that the tradition had created sure paths along which the decision could be reached. But even so, law is no small thing, but always concerned with the most important matter, namely the safeguarding of the community and of justice. The standing of a judge is always of the highest order, quite apart from the actual importance of the matter at issue. It may be asked whether we can venture to reach any verdict concerning the ultimate worth of the Hebrew legal assembly. We need not venture to do so for ourselves, for it lies ready to hand. The prophets speak in no uncertain terms. Their verdict is unfavourable:

[1] Cf. p. 150 n.

'Thus saith Yahweh:
For three transgressions of Israel,
Yea for four, I will not turn away the punishment thereof.
Because they have sold the righteous for silver,
And the needy for a pair of shoes:
They pant after the dust on the head of the small man,
And turn aside the rights of the poor' (Amos 2.6-7).

We find it thus in Amos, and this note of complaint and of protest runs from prophet to prophet. The legal assembly is perfect, so long as it is the assembly of free independent peasants, each approximately equal in possessions, and settles their affairs justly in such a way as to preserve the life of the community. But the eighth century, the time of Amos himself, shows a marked shift in economic circumstances[1] and the beginning of a distinct stratification of Hebrew society. Beside the possessors of land we find those who have no possessions, beside independent citizens we find dependants. At this point the legal assembly fails. The oral and public nature of its conduct of affairs presupposes that each assessor can speak what he thinks right, independently of the others. But fear of those who have economic power and who can do real harm in the narrow common life of the village, makes men subservient and lacking in independence. Anyone who knows the conditions of the countryside knows what a blessing it is that the vote is in writing and secret. Those who suffer from this social division of the Hebrew community are precisely those whose protec-

---

[1] M. Lurje, *Studien zur Geschichte der wirtschaftlichen und sozialen Verhältnisse im israelitisch-jüdischen Reiche* (1927), seems to me to be too much tied to modern views to be able to give a true picture of the state of affairs. A proletariat such as he envisages never did exist among the Hebrews.

tion and defence was the highest pride of the legal assembly, and the sign of its true strength and freedom—the weak, the widows, the orphan still under age, the 'stranger within the gates' who had no civil rights.

> 'Seek judgement,
> Check the violent,
> Give the fatherless his rights,
> Plead the widow's cause' (Isa. 1.17).

All those passages of the prophetic teaching which the nineteenth century described as 'the social gospel of the prophets' and which have had so marked an effect upon the social movements and legal developments of recent times, are rooted in these conditions. Our task is to consider how, because of these conditions, a change came about in the form of the legal assembly. It is not explicitly described, but may be clearly deduced from the sources.

About the year 700, that is, as a sequel to the work of the prophets Amos, Hosea, Micah and Isaiah, a new form of speech begins to appear in the literature of the Old Testament. 'And now, O Israel, hearken unto the statutes and unto the judgements, which I am teaching you to perform, so that you may live, and so that you may enter into possession of the land which Yahweh, the God of your fathers, is intending to give you . . . Keep them and do them. For this will be your wisdom and your understanding in the sight of other peoples. When they hear of all these statutes, they will say: Surely this great nation is a wise and understanding people. For what great nation is there that hath a god so nigh unto them as Yahweh our God is whensoever we call upon him? And what great nation is there, that hath statutes and judgements so perfect as this whole law which I set before you this day?' (Deut. 4.1, 6-8). Who is it who speaks thus, so urgently, so broadly, so much from the heart, warning, promising, presupposing good intentions, repeating again and again what is well known, ethical and religious alike? It is not the prophet. His words are more terse, more definite, more decisive, fresher and more profound in form and content. Nor is it the popular speaker, for he speaks less religiously, more boldly, less clerically, more worldly, less sustainedly. It is the preacher who speaks thus. With the seventh century, the preacher begins to make his voice heard. The sermon, the greatest and best form of human instruction, comes into being. It follows on the prophets, and prepares the way for the transformation of life according to the ideas which the prophets were sent to formulate. It spreads abroad among the population the gold of the revelation, in small change and not always without a certain lowering of value.

In about 700 there began in Judah a great preaching activity which leaves its traces in all the writings of the second half of the seventh century. Where we meet with it, the sermon style is already mature and fully developed. It must therefore have come into being earlier. Preaching is never without a purpose. The purpose of this preaching, whether we examine it in the 'framework' of the book of Judges, or in the amplifications of the book of Jeremiah, or in the introductions to Deuteronomy, is always the education of the people of Judah to zeal for the statutes of God. Its content is drawn from the basic ideas of the proclamation of the prophets—that God is holy, that he controls history, that he demands obedience, that the sum-total of obedience to him is righteousness, social righteousness. Since to these ideas, which are to be found in all the prophets, there are added certain ideas which are only to be found in Isaiah or only to be deduced from his proclamation, namely, that Jerusalem is God's holy city, and the people which worships him in Jerusalem is his holy people, we set the beginning of preaching in the time which follows upon Isaiah. For before this time there was no preaching at all, and the transformation of worship from sacrifice and cultus to preaching and obedience which here begins, marks an enormous spiritualization of piety. For the same reason we suggest that the fathers of this preaching activity are to be found in the priesthood of Jerusalem and of its temple, who for centuries had to struggle for recognition.[1]

From these same priestly circles, when preaching had sufficiently prepared the people and the other conditions were ripe,[2] there issued the book which contained a significant transformation of the Hebrew community of law. This is the fifth book of Moses, the so-called Deuteronomy, brought out into the open in

[1] It would be a fascinating project to examine thoroughly both as to content and style the so-called Deuteronomic passages for which we are claiming this 'sermon' style.

[2] Josiah, the king of Deuteronomy, became king at the age of eight (II Kings 22.1). This explains why he never became completely independent, and so why it was possible to venture under his rule to preserve the kingship only in name, but in reality to make it into a shadow-kingship, as happens in Deut. 17.14 ff. It is indeed hardly credible that anyone later should have inserted such a law, as many assume, whereas this transformation of the king into a *basileus hiereus* fits equally into the situation under Josiah as it corresponds to the removal of that harm which the kingship brought with it. It is quite comprehensible in 625, and therefore genuine.

about 625 and not likely to have been composed much earlier, a writing whose influence on the law-giving of later times, right down to the present day, it would be a worthwhile undertaking to show. This book of Deuteronomy has been called a law-book. The name is not a correct one. It is a collection of laws in which old legal precepts clearly alternate with quite new ones.[1]

Only one single precept concerns us here. 'If there arise a matter too hard for thee for judgment, in matters of bloodshed, or of legal claims, or of mal-treatment, matters of controversy in thy gates: then shalt thou arise, and get thee up into the place which Yahweh thy God shall choose (i.e. Jerusalem); and thou shalt come to the Levitical priests, and to the judges that shall be in those days:[2] and thou shalt inquire (after justice); and they shall declare to thee the legal decision' (17.8-9). Here again we see quite clearly that

[1] It is perhaps necessary to stress to theological readers that the difference between a law-book and a collection of laws is not just a matter of splitting hairs about terms. A law-book is a collection of legal precepts which comes thus into being because the law-giver sets out his individual precepts with the quite definite intention of laying down the law and thus follows a consistent and unified legal principle. A collection of laws, however, lacks just this unified and thorough-going principle of lawgiving and puts together legal precepts old and new which are still to be regarded as valid, so that the fundamental principle of law-giving need not be a unified one, and normally is not thus unified. Thus there still occur to-day in collections of laws, laws which are valid but which are centuries old and have com-pletely changed their meaning as a result of their explanation over this period of time. Deuteronomy cannot be divided into strata by dividing it up according to legal or even stylistic differences. The division of a given work into strata only has meaning (as in the case of the Pentateuch) when as a result we obtain documents which are intelligible in themselves and whose combination together may also be understood. Divisions of Deuteronomy up to date have produced nothing but loose units without rhyme or reason.

[2] This fiction of presenting Moses as the law-giver, or rather as the mediator of law-giving, is an old device.

legal assemblies are presupposed in every settlement. It is further presupposed that certain legal cases are too difficult for these local courts. They are then to be taken to what we to-day should call a single higher court.

Without reading too much into this, we may interpret the precept as follows. The main fault of the legal assembly, according to the prophets, is its social unrighteousness. In matter of fact terms this means that the personal involvement of the assessors in the questions being discussed would often hinder a correct judgment. To this unrighteousness, there may well be added a second deficiency. The marked division of Palestine, whose influence on the rate of exchange of currency I was myself able to observe in 1908,[1] has the result that, just as measures and weights vary, so also does the judgement of individual facts of the case diverge widely in the legal assemblies of the different places and districts. We may compare the divergences in the criminal codes of the different parts of the Swiss federation. But justice is only justice when it is measured everywhere by the same standards. Local prejudice and variations in legal decisions from place to place hamper the evenness of justice. For this reason, Deuteronomy puts an end to the Hebrew community of law by freeing the sources of justice and the work of the magistrates from the restriction of fortuitous local situations, and putting them where the city and the temple dominate, where greater breadth of view and deeper obligation to the God of the prophets prevails, in other words, in Jerusalem.

[1] For one 'beshlik' I received between Jaffa and Smyrna quite arbitrarily different numbers of 'metalliks'.

Thus, and this is a point that the commentators have normally missed, Deuteronomy is at one and the same time a source of the proclamation of the unification of places of worship and of the unification of justice. The old local legal assembly has had its useful period of life and has served its purpose, but now is replaced. There is something more to note here. The introduction of a new collection of laws unites within it two aims. On the one hand it presents the law-givers' conception of ideas which have in the meantime been newly created or have changed. It follows along behind the development of new ideas. On the other hand, however—and to find the right path in this indicates the real wisdom of the law-giver—it deliberately sets out to shape justice, educating men in a deeper and better conception of it. (Any Swiss pastor who studies the cases of trusteeship in Swiss civil law in order to fulfil his duties properly, will come upon intentions of the wise law-giver whose excellence has by no means yet been brought to full effect.) Deuteronomy proceeds very wisely in its striving after unification. It does not attempt to compel it by mere innovation, but cautiously prepares the way for it. It simply creates the possibility of making an appeal to a higher place in difficult cases. But it knows that many legal assemblies will be glad not to have to conduct difficult cases within the local limitations. It will be the most awkward questions which are first brought to Jerusalem. This expedient for the legal assemblies, once adopted, will have its consequence. One law, one righteousness will prevail throughout the whole land, and the ancient complaint of the prophets will be silenced. Whether then the legal assemblies will come to an end, or whether, as is normal in present-day justice, a division of responsibility will be made, may be left for the future to show.

We cannot in fact say what the future did show, for shortly after the introduction of Deuteronomy the exile broke up the Jewish state. The legal system of the returned exiles, of the post-exilic community, rests on quite different presuppositions. It does not depend upon a free national life, but is the jurisdiction of a religious community which is itself a member of a foreign state and is a guest in its own land.

III

I may, perhaps, be permitted a short closing remark of quite a different kind. The significance of the Hebrew legal assembly is not fully presented without this comment. Nothing makes for edification so much as the practice of justice, and to me at least it seems one of the deep failures of the present that the care of justice is deprived of so much of its respect by publicity. There would seem to me to be no nobler task for our newspapers than to give space and energy to the reporting of the conduct of justice and of the great questions of justice in a serious and dignified manner. We can so easily get out of the habit of thinking of justice itself. Then justice degenerates into a mere instrument of utility. It is disastrous for a people to whom that happens. But we may hold ourselves open to the consideration of the ideas and questions of justice with continual attentiveness. Then justice becomes a trust committed to the conscience and to public opinion, which works, as hardly anything else does, to edify and to preserve a people. In this lies the greatest contribution made by the Hebrew legal assembly to the people and spirit of the Old Testament.

The Hebrew thinks in the forms of justice. His ideal is the righteous man. This means primarily the one who, when accused of a crime, is in a position to prove his innocence. It then comes to mean one who carries out justly all the demands of community life. Then it comes to mean the one who gives obedience to the demands of God himself. The righteous man is the pious man. Piety is for the Hebrews not a matter of feeling or of the proper forms, it is a question of moral testing in the sight of the highest judge. For God himself is the God of righteousness. However beautiful, or kindly, or friendly, or joy-bringing the gods of Greece and other lands may be, the God of the Old Testament is righteous. The Hebrew legal assembly did this for Israel, and indeed for mankind, that it made Israel able to appropriate the revelation that God is a God of peace, of fellowship, of righteousness, who demands obedience and continual testing in a kind of behaviour which fits together one's own desires and wishes with the conditions and claims of others. Since we were all born for righteousness, and since there is nothing nobler for a man than to desire only his own rights and not to diminish the rights of any other, since all life, in the smallest and greatest groups, from the family to the comity of nations, can rest on no other foundation than that of justice, the Hebrew legal assembly has a significance which goes far beyond mere cultural history, a significance which affects every one of us.

It would be proper for the theologian to go further here and to point out how, according to the message of the New Testament, it is just this final demand that we should be pious, righteous before God, which lies beyond our own ability and power, so that we must all live by grace. But let this indication of it suffice. Just one phrase from the New Testament may be added, a word whose profundity none can escape. Jesus once said: 'Blessed are they that hunger and thirst after righteousness: for they shall be filled' (Matt. 5.6).

INDEX OF AUTHORS

Abel, 130 n.
Albright, 20 n.
Alt, 144 n., 150 n.
Arias Montano, 12 n.

Benedict, 17 n.
Benzinger, 12
Bertholet, 13
Bertramus, 12 n.
Beza, 12 n.
Boaz, 17 n.
Brunner, 107 n.
Budde, K., 160 n.

Cohn, 151
Cox, 17 n.

Dallas, 13
Dalman, 12 n., 25 n.
Doreid, Ibn, 66 n.
Duhm, B., 53 n., 58
Dussaud, 20 n.

Eichhorn, J. G., 15
Erman, A., 27 n.

Feist, 17 n.
Fishberg, 17 n.
Fries, 159 n.

Galling, 20 n.
Geier, 12 n.
Granqvist, 90 n.

Gressmann, 19 n.
Gülkowitsch, 132 n.
Gunkel, H., 106, 159

Herodotus, 24, 72 f.
Hertzberg, 157 n.
Hess, 26 n., 66 n.

Jahnow, 40 n., 110 n.

Kautzsch, E., 160 n.
Kohler, J., 151
Köhler, L., 14 n., 34 n., 65 n., 68 n., 72 n., 77 n., 84 n., 117 n., 130 n., 153 n., 163 n.
König, E., 160 n.
Kuenen, 159 n.

Lande, 77 n.
Larsen, 43 n.
Littmann, E., 67 n.
Löw, 12 n.
Lurje, 166 n.

Macalister, 21 f., 21 n.
Meissner, 27 n.
Mowinckel, 153 n.
Musil, A., 161 n.

Neumark, 83 n.
Noth, 64 n., 150 n.
Nowack, 12

Osenbrüggen, 151 n.
Ovid, 34 n.

Pedersen, 13
Peters, 159, 160 n.
Ploss, H. H., 37 n.
Poulsen, 43 ń., 50 n.

Ranke, 27 n.
Relandus, 12 n.
Renan, 159
Rieu, 32

Samter, 52 n.
Saulcy, de, 20
Sayce, 19 n.
Schlözer, A. L. von, 15
Schwally, 116 n.
Schwöbel, 149 n.
Sigonius, 12 n.
Steuernagel, C., 160 n.

Ursinus, 12 n.

Winkworth, 83 n.

Xenophon, 34 n.

SUBJECT INDEX

Anxiety, religion of, 143
Apparitions, 111 f.
Aristotle, 133

Barabbas, 64 n.
bar miṣwāh, 87
Beard, 27 f.
Beauty, 32 34
Benjamin, 52
Birth, 49
'Black ones', 135
Blinding, 53
Blindness, 53
Bones, from excavations, 20
Book of the Covenant, 141 f.
Burial, 109 f.
Burning, 112

Calendar, 74 f.
Castration, 39
Casuistry, 143
Cattle thieves, 98
Celibacy, 89
Cephalic index, 18
Chaos, 127 f.
Childlessness, 49
Children's games, 72
Circumcision, 37
Clean and unclean, 143
Community of war, 96 ff.
Confession, 88
Conversation, 99 ff.

Conversational forms, 77
Cosmic insecurity, 128
Counting, 75
Covenant, Book of the, 141 f.
Creation, 125 f.
Cripples, 52
Crouching position, 22
Cultic community, 88
Culture, 126

Daily programme, 99 f.
Daniel, 121
Dante, 82
David story, 82 f.
Dead men, 111 f.
Death, 107
Defilement, 111
Demons, 135
Density of population, 69 f.
Doctor, 53 ff.
'Dry ones', 135

Earthquake, 130, 137
Eclipses, 129 f.
Edomites, 25
Education, 73 ff.
Elijah, 29, 130.
Eunuch, 39 f.
Evil spirits, 135
Excavations, 20
Ezekiel, 142

179

Farmsteads, 69
Female children, 84
Fighting ability, 30, 96 ff.

Grandson, 64 n.
Greeks, 131

Hair, 26 f.
'Hairy ones', 135
ḥākām, 104
Health, 46 f.
Hebrews, 16
Height, 18, 23 f.
Helen of Adiabene, 20
Herodotus, 24, 72 f.
History, 139, 145

Illness, 46 f.
Industries, 74
Infancy, 68
Infant mortality, 42 f.
Insecurity, cosmic, 128
   in life, 129 f.

'Jewish nose', 17
Jews, 17
Job, 58
Jonah, 122
Joseph story, 82

kēf, 100
kosmos, 131

Lament for dead, 110
Landslide, 137
Law, 95 ff., 141 ff., 169 ff.
Lefthandedness, 52
Legal assembly, 151 ff.
Leprosy, 56 ff.

Levites, 45, 74
Life, duration of, 41 ff.
   in open air, 70
   insecurity in, 129 f.
   stages of, 45 f.
Lions, plague of, 97

Male guardianship, 84 f.
Marcus Aurelius, 43
Marriage, 89 f.
Mass emotion, 118
Maturity, 61
Mealtimes, 101 f.
'Mediterranean man', 23
Miracles, 133
Miriam-Mary, 33
Miscarriage, 51, 135
Moses story, 82
Mourning, 110
   —customs, 40, 110
   —period, 110
Murad III, 43

nabis, 118, 123
Names—as talismans, 65
   —occasional, 66
   —protective, 66
   —theophoric, 65
Naming, 63 ff.
Nature, 131 f.
Nausicaa, 32
něphīlīm, 51, 135
Neuroses, 143
Nurse, 68

'ōlām, 132
Old age, complaints of, 48 f.
   —and death, 107 f.

SUBJECT INDEX

Ownership marks, 75

Pathology, 18
Peasant village, 69, 152
pele', 133
Perez, 52
Personal particulars, 67 f.
Place of woman, 84
Plaits, 26
Plato, 107, 154, 159
Pliny, 50, 133
Polygamy, 91 f.
Population, density of, 69 f.
Praise of woman, 73
Preaching, 168
Priesthood, 74
Priestly code, 142
Professions, 74
Prognathism, 22
Proverbs, 104
Psychoses, 19, 143

Race, 15
Reading, 75
Reciters, 82
Reckoning, 75
Religion of anxiety, 143
Rheumatism, 22, 59
Romans, 131 f.

Sacrificial festival, 88
Safety, 137
ṣārāh, 92
ṣāra'at, 56
School, 77
Scribes, 76
Script, 76
Self-mutilation, 40

Semitic, 15
Sensitivity, 122
Sheol, 113
Shepherd life, 97
Skin, colour, 24 ff.
—disease, 55 ff.
Socrates, 107, 154
sōd, 99, 102
Solitude, 137
Spoken story, 33
Stages of life, 45 f.
Stoning, 112
Stories, 33, 81
Storytellers, 80, 103
Sunstroke, 54

Tamar, 32
Terror, 134
Thomas, 64 n.
Tradition, 138 ff., 145

Undernourishment, 59

Vitiligo, 57

War, community of, 96 ff.
Watchman, 101
Weaning, 68
Weeping, 110 f.
Wife, choice of, 90 f.
Woman, place of, 84
—praise of, 73
Work, capacity for, 71
World view, 131
Writing, 75

Zobeba, 33

INDEX OF BIBLICAL REFERENCES

Bible Ref.	Page	Bible Ref.	Page
Genesis		Genesis—cont.	
1.1-2.4	41 n., 125	21.5	41 n.
1.2	127	21.8	68
1.3 f., 6 f.	128 n.	24	16
1.9	128 n.	24.30-34	33
1.11-25	133	24.48	90
1.26	34	25.1 ff., 7	93
1.26 f.	126	25.8	109
1.28	50, 89, 126	25.21 ff.	49
2.4 ff.	125	25.25	25
2.24, 3.16	89	25.26	41 n.
4.25	64 n.	27.1	108
5	41	27.11, 23	28
5.31	41	27.21	48
6.3	45	29	64, 91
6.4	51, 135	29.17	34
7.6	41	29.23, 28	16
8.22	129	30	64
9.29	41	30.1	49, 89
10	15	30.1-4	49
11.10-32	41 n.	30.9-14	49
11.30	49	30.14-17	50
12.11	34	34	38
16	93	34.1-4	91
16.1 f.	49	35.8	68
17	87	35.18	52
17.1-14	37	35.25 f.	93
17.7 f.	144	35.29	109
17.24 f.	38	38.6	32
17.25	87	38.29	52
18.13	107	39.6	34
19.31	141	41.50 ff.	16
20.9, 11	141	47.9, 28	41 n.
20.12	90	48.5 f.	16
20.17 f.	49	48.10	48

183

Bible Ref.	Page	Bible Ref.	Page
Genesis—cont.		*Numbers—cont.*	
49.29	110	8.24, 26	45
50.10	110	11.25	118
		12.1	16, 93
Exodus		13.32 f.	24
1.19	29	13.33	51, 135
2.3-9	68	14.29	45, 61
3.1-3	134	14.33	45
4.25	38	27.1-11	158 n.
6.7	144	32.11	45, 61
12.26 ff.	79	33.39	43
12.40	41 n.		
12.43-49	38	Deuteronomy	
13.9, 16	140	1.28	24
15.26	55	2.10	24
18.1	39	4.1, 6-8	168
20.5	62	4.9	79 f.
20.12	108	5.16	108
20.24-23.12	141	6.7, 20 f.	80
21.9	157 n.	9.2	24
21.22	51	11.19	80
23.28 f.	117	11.23	24
		14.1	40
Leviticus		17.8 f.	170
10.6	27	17.14 ff.	169 n.
13	56 f., 60	20.1-9	116
13.4 f., 21 ff.	57	21.10-14	93
17.7	135	21.18-21	109, 164 n.
18	94	23.1 [Heb. 2]	39 f.
18.9	90	32.11	127
18.18	92	32.17	135
19.32	108	32.25	28
21	111	33.25	28
21.19	53	34.7	43, 48
22.4, 8	89		
27.1-8	45	Joshua	
		5.2 ff.	38
Numbers		6.21	27
4.3	45	14.10	43 f.
6.5	27	24.29	43

INDEX OF BIBLICAL REFERENCES

Bible Ref.	Page	Bible Ref.	Page
Judges		I Samuel—*cont.*	
3.15	52	30.21-25	158 n.
5.2	26		
13.2	49	II Samuel	
14.5 f.	29	1.23	29
15.18	39	2.18	29
16.13 f.	26	3.2-5	92
16.16	123	3.15 f.	91
17	74	3.29	44
19.1-10	90	4.4	53, 73
20.16	52	5.14	64 n.
		6.23	49
I Samuel		11.2	34
1.1-7	49, 92	12.1 ff.	164 n.
1.21 ff.	68	12.7	120
2.6 f.	83	12.15-23	121
2.13	157 n.	13.1-15	91
2.31 f.	44	13.1	32
3.2	48	13.2	123
4.15	43	13.13	90
8.9	157 n.	14.1 ff.	164 n.
8.20	165	14.26	27
9.9	11	14.27	32, 34
10.5	118	15.1-6	164 n.
10.23	24	19.32 [Heb. 33]	44
11.5 ff.	98	19.35-37 [Heb. 36-38]	108
11.7	119	20.1 f.	118
16.12	25	23.20	29, 97
16.18	30, 78		
17.4	24	I Kings	
17.34-36	29	1-2	109
17.34-37	96	1.1-4	48
17.42	25, 34	2.2	109
18.20 f.	91	2.26 f.	74
19.20-24	118	4.25 [Heb. 5.5]	100
21.5	56	4.28 [Heb. 5.8]	157 n.
21.5 f.	88	9.8	136 f.
25.25	66	11.1-8	92
25.44	91	14.1-6	54
28	111	14.4	48

Bible Ref.	Page	Bible Ref.	Page
I Kings—cont.		Isaiah—cont.	
		38.21 f.	54
17.1	130	46.4	109
18.1-19.4	123	51.9-11	140
18.28	40, 157 n.	51.17, 22	11
18.46	29	53.2 f.	34
22.6	118	65.20	45
22.7-28	119		
22.34 f.	29	Jeremiah	
		1.1	74
II Kings		1.4-10	120
1.1-8	54	1.5	89
2.19-22	51	4.4	39
2.23 ff.	73	4.19 f.	51
4.8-17	50	5.22	128
4.18 ff.	54	15.17	89, 102
5	54, 57	16.2	89
7.3 ff.	56	19.8	137
8.7-9	54	26	154
17.27	97	26.17-19	157
22.1	169 n.	35.5	11
24.17	64	39.7	53
25.7	53	50.39	136
Isaiah			
1.2	43	Ezekiel	
1.14	123	13.9	102
1.17	157, 167	14.12 ff.	58
2.3	144	32.27	51
2.4	148	44.20	27
5.1-7	69		
13.7 f.	130	Hosea	
13.10	129	2.16 f. [Heb. 18 f.]	147
13.20 ff.	136	7.9	107
13.21	135 f.		
18.2, 7	24	Joel	
21.11	101	2.7	29
23.13	136		
28.10-12	120	Amos	
28.26, 29	139	1.1	131
34.14	135 f.	2.6-7	166

INDEX OF BIBLICAL REFERENCES 187

Bible Ref.	Page	Bible Ref.	Page
Amos—*cont.*		Psalms—*cont.*	
3.8	97	58.8 [Heb. 9]	51
3.12	98	65.7 [Heb. 8]	128
6.9-11	58	72.7	131 n.
6.10	109	90.10	45
7.10-17	120	91.6	135
		106.37	135
Jonah		111.1	102
2.5 [Heb. 6]	128 n.	113-118	102 n.
4.2 f.	123	121.8	69, 153
		124.4 f.	128 n.
Zephaniah		127.3	50
1.8	74	147.10	29
2.13 ff.	136		
3.5	154	Proverbs	
		2.20	141
Zechariah		13.12	123
8.4	48	14.34	148
8.5	72	17.22	123
13.6	40	25.20 LXX	106
14.4	11	26.3	106
		26.7	52, 106
Malachi		26.11, 14 f.	106
1.11	144	30.7 f.	105
2.11	16	30.18 f.	105
2.13	111	31.10-31	73
2.15	94		
		Job	
Psalms		3-31	158
1.2	101	3.16	51
1.5	155	3.20, 22	158
6.5 [Heb. 6]	113	6.14 f., 24 f.	161
7.8 [Heb. 9]	157	8.2	161
15	88	11.2 f.; 12.2 f.	162
19.5 [Heb. 6]	38	13.4	53
26.1	157	15.2 f.; 16.2-4	162
30 Title [Heb. v. 1]	142	31	158
35.24	157	31.7 f., 21 f.	160
43.1	157	31.35	75 n., 160,
45.2 [Heb. 3]	34	42.17	27, 109

Bible Ref.	Page	Bible Ref.	Page
Song of Songs		II Chronicles	
1.5 f.	26	11.15	135
4.1	26	13.21	92
5.11	26	21.12-15	54
6.5	26		
7.7 f. [Heb. 8 f.]	32	Tobit	
		2.10	53
Ruth			
1.20	84	Ecclesiasticus	
4.1 f.	151	18.9	45
4.2	155		
4.16	84 n.	Matthew	
4.17	85	5.6	175
		5.8	148
Ecclesiastes		21.15	72
6.3	51	26.30	102 n.
12.1-6	49		
		Mark	
Lamentations		1.35	137
2.15	137	5.5	60
		5.40	54
Esther			
1.11	34	Luke	
2.3, 14 f.	40	1.52 f.	83
4.4	40	2.10	134
		3.23	63
Daniel		12.19	30
1.4	31	15.8	71
1.8-15	34	17.12-17	57
3.1-18	121		
		John	
Nehemiah		12.32 f.	12 n.
4.16 ff. [Heb. 10 ff.]	99	16.33	138
13.23 f.	16	21.18 f.	12. n.
13.24	73		
		Acts	
I Chronicles		5.1-10	110
2.18	64 n.		
4.8	33	Romans	
6.24 [Heb. 9]	64 n.	14.17	148
23.1	109		
23.24	45		

Bible Ref.	Page	Bible Ref.	Page
I Corinthians		James	
15.8	51	5.17	130 n.
Galatians		I Peter	
2	39	2.9	133
I Timothy			
2.15	49, 89		